CHRISTMAS COOKIE MURDER

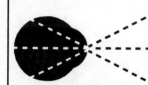

This Large Print Book carries the
Seal of Approval of N.A.V.H.

A LUCY STONE MYSTERY

CHRISTMAS COOKIE MURDER

WITHDRAWN

LESLIE MEIER

WHEELER PUBLISHING
A part of Gale, Cengage Learning

GALE
CENGAGE Learning

Detroit • New York • San Francisco • New Haven, Conn • Waterville, Maine • London

LARGE TYPE
m MEIER, L

GALE
CENGAGE Learning

Copyright © 1999 by Leslie Meier.
Wheeler Publishing, a part of Gale, Cengage Learning.

LIBRARY OF CONGRESS CATALOGING-IN-PUBLICATION DATA

Meier, Leslie.
  Christmas cookie murder : a Lucy Stone mystery / by Leslie
Meier.
    p. cm.
  ISBN-13: 978-1-59722-859-6 (pbk. : alk. paper)
  ISBN-10: 1-59722-859-1 (pbk. : alk. paper)
  1. Stone, Lucy (Fictitious character)—Fiction. 2. Women
detectives—Maine—Fiction. 3. Reporters and
reporting—Fiction. 4. Young women—Crimes against—Fiction.
5. Christmas—Maine—Fiction. 6. Community life—Fiction. 7.
Maine—Fiction. 8. Large type books. I. Title.
PS3563.E3455C56 2008
813'.54—dc22   2008032222

Published in 2008 by arrangement with Kensington Books, an imprint
of Kensington Publishing Corp.

CHRISTMAS COOKIE MURDER

CHAPTER ONE

28 days 'til Xmas

"I'd rather die."

Judging by her determined expression and her firm tone of voice, Lucy Stone was pretty sure that her best friend, Sue Finch, had made up her mind. Still, ever the optimist, she couldn't resist trying one last time.

"Oh, come on," pleaded Lucy. "It won't seem like Christmas without it."

"Nope." Sue shook her head and shoved a piece of overpriced lettuce around her plate with a fork. "No cookie exchange this year."

The two friends were having lunch at the Chandlery, the toney bistro in the Ropewalk, the newest mall in Tinker's Cove. The Ropewalk had once been exactly that, a nineteenth-century workshop complete with a long, narrow alley used for twisting hemp fibers into rope for the clipper ships that once sailed all over the globe from their home port in Tinker's Cove, Maine.

Long a ramshackle eyesore on the waterfront, it had recently been restored, and local craftsmen had moved in, creating what the developer called "an exciting retail adventure with a seafaring ambiance."

Today, the day after Thanksgiving, the Ropewalk was packed with Christmas shoppers and Lucy and Sue had had to wait thirty minutes for a table. When their salads finally came they were definitely on the skimpy side — the kitchen was obviously running low on supplies. The two friends hadn't minded; the demands of juggling homes and careers made it difficult for them to spend time together, and they were enjoying each other's company.

"It's not like it was, well, even a few years ago," said Sue. "Then we were all in the same boat. We all had little kids and plenty of time on our hands. People snapped up the invitations and brought wonderful cookies." A dreamy expression came over her face. "Remember Helen's baklava?"

"Do I ever," said Lucy, who had a round face and a shining cap of hair cut in a practical style. She was casually dressed, wearing a plaid shirt-jacket and a pair of well-worn jeans. "It was like biting into a little piece of heaven." She paused and sipped her coffee. "Whatever happened to her?"

"She moved away, to North Carolina, I think," said Sue, who provided an elegant contrast to her friend in her hand-knit designer sweater and tailored flannel slacks. "And that's exactly my point. A lot of the old regulars have moved away. And things have changed. Getting together to compare recipes and swap cookies isn't as appealing as it used to be."

"It is to me," said Lucy. "I've still got a family to feed, and they don't think it's Christmas without cookies. Lots of different kinds. I don't have time to bake five or six batches. And to be honest, I don't want to have that many cookies around the house." She bit her lip. "Too much temptation. Too many calories."

"I know," Sue said with a sigh. "With the exchange you just had to bake one double batch."

"But you ended up with twelve different kinds, a half dozen of each." Lucy started counting them off on her fingers. "Your pecan meltaways, my Santa's thumbprints, spritz, gingerbread men, Franny's Chinese-noodle cookies, shortbread, and Marge's little pink-and-white candy canes. . . ."

"Marge probably can't come this year,"

said Sue, with a sad shake of her head. "The lumpectomy wasn't enough, and they've started her on chemotherapy. She feels lousy."

"I hadn't heard," said Lucy, furrowing her brow. "That's too bad."

"I thought you newspaper reporters thrived on local gossip," teased Sue, referring to Lucy's part-time job writing for the weekly *Pennysaver.*

"Actually, I'm so busy covering historic commission hearings and stuff like that, I never have time to call my friends." She smiled at Sue and glanced around at the restaurant, which was festively decorated with artificial pine garlands, ribbons, and gold balls. "This is fun — we don't get together enough. So what else is new? Fill me in."

"Have you heard about Lee?"

"Lee Cummings? No. What?"

"Well," began Sue, leaning across the table toward Lucy, "she and Steve have separated."

"You're kidding." Lucy was astonished. Lee and her husband, dentist Steve Cummings, had seemed a rock-solid couple. They went to church together every Sunday, and Steve had coached his daughter's T-ball team.

"No." Sue's eyebrows shot up. "Apparently Steve is finding marriage too confining. At least that's what Lee says."

"She tells you all this?"

"Oh, yes. And more. Every morning when she drops Hillary off at the center." Sue directed the town's day-care center, located in the basement of the recreation building. "It's all she can talk about. Steve did this. Steve did that. His lawyer says this. My lawyer says that. The latest is who's going to get the stove."

"They're arguing over the stove?"

"I think it's a Viking," explained Sue, with a knowing nod. "But that's just the beginning. They're also fighting over the books and the CDs and the china and the stupid jelly glasses with cartoon characters."

"So you think they're going to get a divorce?"

"It sure looks that way."

"And that's all she talks about?"

"Yeah. And if I have the cookie exchange, I'll have to invite her, and if she comes, she'll turn the whole evening into a group-therapy session. Trust me on this."

"I can see that's a problem," admitted Lucy, picking up the check. "Come on. Let's get out of here. When the going gets tough, the tough go shopping."

■ ■ ■ ■

Leaving the restaurant and entering the shopping area, the two friends joined the throng that was flowing past the gaily decorated craftsmen's booths. It was crowded, but people were in good humor, aided by the Christmas carols playing on the sound system.

"Tra la la la la, la la la la!" warbled Lucy, unable to resist singing along. "Isn't it nice to hear the carols? They always take me back to my childhood."

"You'll be sick of them soon enough," grumbled Sue. "You know which one I hate? That one about the little drummer boy. Talk about insipid!"

"You're really having an attack of Grinch-itis, aren't you?" asked Lucy, stepping into a booth filled with baskets of potpourri. "Look at these," she said, picking up a package of three padded hangers. "And they smell so good. Do you think Bill's mom would like them?"

"Sure."

"Are they enough? It's kind of skimpy for a Christmas present."

"Add some drawer paper, or sachets," suggested Sue, as a smiling salesclerk approached.

"They're handmade, and filled with our unique blend of potpourri," said the clerk, with an encouraging nod.

Lucy examined the price tag, and her eyes grew large.

"I don't know," she said, hesitating. "What if the scent clashes with her perfume?"

"You wouldn't want that," agreed Sue, who loved to shop but rarely paid full price, preferring to keep an eye out for sales. She could spot a markdown a mile away.

Lucy gave the clerk an apologetic little smile, and the two left the stall. In the walkway outside, Lucy grabbed Sue's arm.

"Did you see the price?" sputtered Lucy. "Thirty-five dollars for three hangers. I can't afford that."

"You're not the only one," said Sue glumly. "I don't think this is going to be a very happy Christmas season. Money's too tight."

"Isn't it always this time of year?"

"This year's worse," said Sue, pausing to examine some handcrafted wooden picture frames. "I've never seen it so bad. I've already gotten a restraining order, and it's only Thanksgiving."

"Restraining order?"

"Yeah. The moms at the center get them

when the dads and boyfriends start acting up. There's always one or two during the holidays, but I've never had one quite so early."

"But the economy's supposed to be booming."

"Not for some of the families using the day-care center. I keep hearing about the lobster quota."

"The state had to do that, or there won't be any lobsters left," said Lucy. "They have to protect the breeding population. I wrote a story about it for the paper."

"I know," agreed Sue, replacing the frame and moving on to the next booth. "But a lot of people in this town depend on lobsters for a living. They're really taking a hit."

"Hi, Franny!" exclaimed Lucy, waving to the woman in the next booth. "I didn't know you'd gone into business."

Franny Small, a fiftyish woman with tightly permed hair, beamed at them proudly from behind a display of jewelry.

"Well, you know, the hardware store finally closed — couldn't compete with that new Home Depot. I was cleaning out the place, and I didn't know what to do with all the bits and pieces — you know nuts and bolts and stuff like that — and then I had this idea to make jewelry. And well, here I am."

"This is hardware?" Lucy looked more closely at a pair of earrings.

"See — that's a hex nut. But these are my favorites — they're dragonflies made from wing nuts. The wings are copper screening."

"Look at that, Sue. Aren't they great?"

"They're wonderful," exclaimed Sue, "and only ten dollars. I'm going to buy a pair to put in Sidra's stocking."

Sidra was Sue's daughter, recently graduated from college and now working as an assistant producer at a TV station in New York.

"That's a good idea," said Lucy, thinking of her own teenage daughter. "I'll get a pair for Elizabeth. She'll love them."

"Do you want them gift-wrapped? I use the old brown paper and string from the store — it kind of completes the look."

"Sure," said Lucy. "Thanks."

"So, Sue, when is the cookie exchange?" asked Franny, as she tore a sheet of paper from the antique roller salvaged from the hardware store. "I want to be sure to mark my calendar."

Sue groaned and Lucy explained. "She says she isn't having it this year."

"That's too bad," said Franny, neatly folding the paper so she didn't have to use tape, and tying the whole thing together with a length of red-and-white string. "Why not?"

"It just didn't seem like such a good idea — I didn't really know who to invite. So many of the old regulars have moved away, and Marge is sick, and . . ."

"Can't you invite some new people?" asked Franny brightly.

"Yeah, Sue," said Lucy, pulling out her wallet. "How about inviting some new people? You must know a lot of nice young moms from the day-care center."

"I'd love to make some new friends," said Franny, giving them their change and receipts. "I don't have much time for myself, what with making the jewelry and running the shop here. I've really been too busy to socialize. I've been looking forward to the cookie exchange for months."

"I knew this was coming," protested Sue. "New people! You don't understand. These young moms aren't like we were. They don't cook! They buy takeout and frozen stuff. Remember when I invited Krissy, the girl who owns that gym? She brought rice cakes! Somehow she didn't get the idea of a cookie exchange at all."

"They were chocolate-chip rice cakes," said Lucy, grinning at the memory.

"Put yourself in their shoes," said Franny, earnestly. "It must be very hard to raise a family and keep a job — I don't know how these young girls do it all."

"With a lot of help from me," muttered Sue. "It isn't just day care, you know. It's advice, and giving them a shoulder to cry on, and collecting toys and clothes and passing them on to the ones who need them."

"You do a fantastic job," said Lucy.

"You do," agreed Franny, turning to help another customer. "But I hope you won't give up the cookie exchange. I'd really miss it."

Lucy gave her a little wave, and they turned to investigate the pottery in the next booth. Lucy picked up a mug, running her fingers over the smooth shape. Then she looked at Sue, who was examining an apple-baker.

"There's no way around it. You have to have the cookie exchange. People are counting on you. It wouldn't be Christmas without it."

Sue's dark hair fell across her face at an angle, and Lucy couldn't see her expression. She hoped she hadn't been too persistent, that she hadn't pushed Sue too hard. She really valued their friendship and didn't want to jeopardize it. When Sue flicked the hair out of her eyes, Lucy was relieved to see that she was smiling.

"You're right, Lucy. It wouldn't be Christmas without the cookie exchange. But it doesn't have to be at my house. Why don't you be the hostess for a change?"

"Me?" Lucy's eyebrows shot up.

"Yup." Sue pointed a perfectly manicured finger at Lucy. "You."

CHAPTER TWO

16 days 'til Xmas

Sue had been right, thought Lucy, pushing open the kitchen door and surveying the mess. Agreeing to host the cookie exchange had been a big mistake. It was almost five o'clock, the guests were due at seven, and she hadn't had a chance to do a thing with the house.

She'd been tied up at *The Pennysaver* all day; she'd spent the morning writing up an interview with Santa, instead of eating lunch she'd dashed out to the Coast Guard station to photograph the guardsmen hanging a huge wreath on the lighthouse and then had gone to the weekly meeting of the Tinker's Cove board of selectmen. The selectmen had been unusually argumentative, which made for good copy, but she wouldn't have a chance to write it up until tomorrow morning, just before the Wednesday noon deadline.

Congratulating herself on her foresight for baking the Dee-Liteful Wine Cake ahead of time, she shrugged off her coat and dropped her notebook on the pile of papers covering the round, golden oak kitchen table. It consisted mostly of financial-aid applications for her oldest child, Toby. He was a high school senior and was applying to several high-priced liberal arts colleges.

He wouldn't be able to go unless he got financial aid, and she had to fill out the complicated forms before January 1, the date recommended by the school guidance office. The thought of the forms was enough to make her feel overwhelmed — how was she supposed to know what their household income would be next year? Bill was a self-employed restoration carpenter, and his earnings varied drastically from year to year. So did hers, for that matter. Ted, the publisher of *The Pennysaver,* only called her when he needed her. She usually worked quite a lot in December, and in the summer months, but things were pretty quiet in coastal Maine in January and February.

First things first, thought Lucy, scooping all the papers into a shopping bag and stuffing it in the pantry. She had to come up with something for dinner, and the sink and counter were covered with dirty dishes.

She opened the door to the family room, and spotted her sixteen-year-old daughter, Elizabeth, stretched out on the couch with her ear to the telephone.

"Elizabeth!" she yelled. "Say good-bye and get in here."

Then she pulled a big stockpot out of the cupboard and filled it with water. She was setting it on the stove when Elizabeth floated in.

"I wish you wouldn't yell when I'm talking to my friends," she complained. "It sounds so low-class."

Lucy gave her a sideways glance. This was something new, she thought. In the past, Elizabeth had concentrated on outraging her parents, insisting on cutting her dark hair into short spikes and threatening to get her nose pierced. Now, Lucy noticed, the black oversize sweater and Doc Martens were gone, replaced by a shiny spandex top with a racing stripe down the side and a pair of sneakers with blue stripes. Her hair was combed into a smooth bob.

"What's with the new look?" asked Lucy.

"Styles change," said Elizabeth, with a shrug. "So what did you want me for?"

"Would you please do something with those dirty dishes? That's supposed to be your responsibility. It's not fair for me to work all day and come home to a messy kitchen."

"It's not my fault," said Elizabeth, demurely folding her hands in front of her. "Toby didn't clean out the dishwasher. It's full, so I had no place to put the dirty dishes."

"Elizabeth, I don't have time for this." Lucy bent down and pulled a can of dusting spray and a rag out from under the sink. "The cookie exchange is tonight; I have a dozen friends coming at seven. So do whatever you have to do, but get this mess cleaned up."

"Okay," said Elizabeth, in a resigned voice. "But it's not fair."

Lucy sighed and charged into the dining room, intending to give the table a quick wipe with the dustcloth. Unfortunately, it was covered with Toby's college applications.

"Toby!" she hollered, aiming her voice in the direction of the hall staircase. "Get down here!"

"He can't hear you. He's got his earphones on," advised eleven-year-old Sara, who was doing homework in the adjacent living room. "What's for dinner?"

"Spaghetti," said Lucy, gathering up the applications and stuffing them in the sideboard. "Be a sweetie and make the salad?"

"Do I have to?" groaned Sara. "I don't feel very good. I think I might be getting my period."

"Really?" asked Lucy, with a surge of interest. "Do you have cramps?"

"No," admitted Sara, who was anxiously awaiting the day when she would join her friends who had already begun menstruating. "I just feel bloated."

"Well, that's probably the stuff you've been eating all afternoon. There's enough dirty dishes in the kitchen to have fed an army. Now scoot and get started on that salad. I've got company coming tonight."

"All I had was yogurt," sniffed Sara, pushing open the door to the kitchen.

"And cereal, and a peanut butter and jelly sandwich, and about a gallon of milk," added Elizabeth, whose head was stuck in the dishwasher. "You're going to get fat if you don't watch it."

"Well, that's better than . . ." began Sara, but the door shut before Lucy could hear the end of the sentence.

Finishing up in the dining room, Lucy flicked her dust cloth around the living room, plumped the couch cushions, and headed for the family room. There she found her youngest child, Zoe, deeply absorbed in a coloring book.

"What'cha doing?" asked Lucy, giving her a little pat on the head.

"Homework."

"I didn't know they had homework in kindergarten, even all-day kindergarten."

Lucy sent up a quick prayer of thanks for the all-day kindergarten program, which had just begun that year. It made it possible for her to work because Zoe now came home on the school bus with her older brother and sisters.

"Let me see that," said Lucy, taking the book. She was amused to see that Zoe had neatly written her name in the upper left-hand corner of the picture, just as she had been taught in school. "Very nice letters."

"The z is hard," said Zoe, very seriously.

"You got it perfect," said Lucy. "Now, would you do me a big favor and set the table for supper?"

"Sure, Mommy."

Lucy sighed. If only they would stay this sweet and agreeable throughout adolescence.

"Thank you, honey," she said, watching fondly as Zoe trotted into the kitchen.

She quickly straightened up the untidy newspapers and magazines, and scooped up a few stray glasses and dishes and carried them into the kitchen.

"How's the salad coming?"

"All done."

"Great. You can help Zoe set the table, okay? Elizabeth, here's some more stuff for the dishwasher and . . ." Lucy stopped in the middle of the room and slapped her hand to her head. "What am I doing?"

"Dinner," reminded Elizabeth.

"Right. Dinner. Did I defrost the hamburger?" She peered in the refrigerator. "No. Of course not." She pulled a package out of the freezer, unwrapped it, and dropped it in the frying pan with a clunk.

"What? No meatballs?" It was Bill, home from work.

"Not tonight." She tilted her cheek up for a kiss and smiled at the tickly feeling from his beard. "I'm kind of frantic, actually," she explained, pushing the meat around with a spatula. "I had to work all day, and the cookie exchange is tonight."

"I thought Sue did that," said Bill, hanging up his coat on the hook by the door.

"I got drafted this year."

"Well, it's a worthy cause — Christmas cookies!" Bill was settling down at the half-set kitchen table, with a cold beer in his hand.

"Since you feel that way, do you mind

finishing up this sauce?" Lucy glanced nervously at the clock on the wall above the stove. "I'd like to set out the party refreshments in the dining room."

"Sure thing." Bill took the spatula from her, and Lucy scurried into the pantry, pulling out the ladder and climbing up to take the cake box off the top shelf. She carried it into the dining room and lifted off the top, expecting to see the festively decorated Dee-Liteful Wine Cake she had stored there.

Instead, she saw that only three-quarters of the cake was left.

Clenching her fists, she marched up the kitchen stairs and threw open the door to Toby's room.

"How could you?" she demanded, pulling off his earphones.

Startled, Toby looked up.

"How could I what?"

"You know what! Eat my cake!"

"What cake?" muttered Toby, grabbing for the earphones.

"The one with sprigs of holly and red candied cherries that was on the top shelf of the pantry." Lucy's arms were akimbo, and she was drumming her fingers against her hips.

"Oh, that one," said Toby, biting his lower lip. Then his face brightened as he turned on the charm. "It's pretty good, Mom."

"Flattery isn't going to get you out of this, buddy," said Lucy, implacably. "What were you thinking? I made a cake and decorated it for you to enjoy all by yourself?"

He lowered his head. "I'm sorry, Mom. I shouldn't have done it. But I was so hungry. It's all this pressure with the college applications and everything."

"Give me a break," muttered Lucy, disgusted. "I'm gonna get you for this — I don't know exactly how, but you'll pay."

She thumped down the front stairs to the dining room and got a knife out of a drawer, cutting the cake into neat slices and arranging them on a plate. She opened a package of holiday napkins, unfolding one and laying it over the sliced cake and arranging the rest on the sideboard, along with her sterling-silver dessert forks and teaspoons, her best china plates and cups and saucers.

Stepping back, she glanced around the room. It wasn't as lavishly decorated as Sue's house, but it was festive. A bowl of holly sat on the sideboard, little electric candles stood on the windowsills, and there was a crystal bowl filled with silver and gold Christmas balls in the middle of the now gleaming mahogany table. She took a deep breath and went from window to window

27

flicking on the candles. She dimmed the overhead chandelier and went into the kitchen to see how dinner was coming.

Bill was just setting a big pot filled with noodles and sauce on the table when Lucy pushed open the kitchen door and slipped into her seat next to Zoe. With impeccable timing, Toby thundered down the back stairs and thumped into his chair.

"Hey, did you hear?" he began, in an effort to deflect her attention from himself. "Richie got into Harvard."

"He did?" Lucy stopped, serving spoon in midair. "How does he know already?"

"Early decision," said Toby, passing the salad bowl.

"Bob and Rachel must be so pleased," said Lucy, wishing that she felt a little more pleased with her own son.

"I bet it costs a pretty penny to go there," said Bill, taking a piece of Italian bread and passing the basket to Lucy.

"I think they're all about the same," said Lucy, busy buttering her bread. "Thirty thousand."

"I just don't get it," complained Bill. "When I went to college it was fifteen hundred a year, and that was everything. Tuition, room and board, the whole she-

bang. I had a five-hundred-dollar scholarship, and Mom got a part-time job to pay
the rest."

"Well, I've got a part-time job," said Lucy.
"But I sure don't make thirty thousand dollars. Most people around here don't even
make that with a full-time job."

"What's the matter with the state college?
That's what I want to know," demanded
Bill, turning toward Toby.

"I'm applying there, too," said Toby,
shoveling a big forkful of spaghetti into his
mouth. "But my guidance counselor says I
should try some of these other schools, too."

"I think we'll qualify for financial aid,"
said Lucy, hoping to ease the tension that
was building up between father and son.

"Well, frankly, before I break my butt trying to pay for a fancy education for the
young prince here, I'd like to see a little
more initiative, if you know what I mean."
Bill gestured angrily with his fork. "His
room's a mess, if you let him he'll sleep until
two or three in the afternoon, and when he
borrows my truck he always brings it back
with an empty gas tank."

Toby didn't respond, but kept his head
down, steadily scooping up his spaghetti.

"You know what I did today?" said Lucy
brightly, changing the subject. "I inter-

viewed Santa Claus!"

"The real Santa Claus?" Zoe was skeptical.

"I think so. It was the Santa at the Ropewalk. It didn't seem polite to ask for his credentials."

"I don't suppose you need a driver's license for a sleigh and reindeer, anyway," observed Elizabeth, who was the proud possessor of a learner's permit.

"What did he say?" asked Zoe.

"Well, he said it's very warm here, compared with the North Pole."

Bill chuckled. "The North Pole is probably the only place colder than here."

"That's exactly why I don't want to go to the state college! I want to get out of this freezing cold place where there's nothing to do," exploded Toby, who had been on a slow simmer. He threw down his napkin and marched out of the room.

"I wish you wouldn't be quite so hard on him," said Lucy.

"I wouldn't have to if you didn't spoil him, now would I?" said Bill.

"So, Sara, how was your day?" asked Lucy, determined to get through the meal with some semblance of civility.

"We had an assembly. A man came who used to be a drug addict. He told us how he ate food from garbage cans and . . ."

"Drugs are terrible," said Lucy. "What made him decide to give them up?"

"Well, he had really hit bottom. He was lying with his face in a pool of vomit . . ."

"Do you mind? We're having dinner," complained Elizabeth.

"Well, Mom asked. I'm only telling what he said."

"I think we get the idea," said Lucy, glancing at the old Regulator clock that hung on the wall. It was almost six-thirty, she had to get a move on. "You girls can clean up and have some frozen yogurt for dessert. I've got to change my clothes."

Hauling herself up the steep back stairway took every bit of energy that Lucy had. She had to concentrate to lift her feet from one step to the next. It had been a long day, she thought, but she wasn't usually this tired. No, it wasn't tiredness, she realized; it was depression.

She pushed open the door to the room she shared with Bill and flicked on a lamp. It was peaceful up here; she could just barely hear the girls' voices in the kitchen downstairs as they squabbled their way through the dishes.

The dormered room was spacious and uncluttered. The dresser tops were neatly

31

organized, a rocking chair in the corner held only a needlepoint cushion and the wood grain of the blanket chest gleamed in the lamplight. The bed was neatly made, covered with a white woven bedspread.

It looked so inviting, thought Lucy. It wouldn't hurt to stretch out for a minute or two, just to put her feet up and rest her eyes.

Falling back on the pillows, Lucy stretched her arms and legs and made a conscious effort to relax. She tried to push the dark clouds from her mind and to think of the enjoyable evening ahead. But instead, she kept replaying Bill's voice. His tone had been so antagonistic, calling Toby "the young prince." What was that all about?

Sure, Toby was lazy and liked to sleep late on weekends. And he was messy, but no more so than his friends. But, to give him credit, he was a pretty good kid. He got all As and Bs in school, he had been captain of the soccer team this fall and he'd scored an impressive 1450 on his SATs.

With that package and any luck at all, thought Lucy, feeling her spirits brightening a little, he would get into a really good college. Oh, probably not Ivy League like Richie, but he could certainly get into one of the top twenty liberal arts colleges. Which would it be? He had shown interest in Amherst and Williams, and of course there were Bates and Bowdoin and Colby right here in Maine.

Wasn't it lucky, she thought, that she had a new car. A fire had totaled her old Subaru wagon, and she had a spiffy new model. It would look great with a classy college decal on the back window. Of course, she thought, with a little pang of jealousy, her sticker wouldn't be quite as prestigious as Rachel's Harvard sticker. But then, Rachel had to put her sticker on a very elderly, rusty Volvo.

She suddenly felt much better, she realized, hopping off the bed. She'd talk to Bill and find out what was bothering him. But down deep, she knew, he wanted the best for Toby just as much as she did.

Lucy opened a drawer and took out a bright red sweatshirt with a huge Santa printed on the front. Just looking at the ridiculous thing made her smile; it had been a gift from Zoe last Christmas. There weren't too many occasions that it was suitable for, but it would be perfect for the cookie exchange. She took off the plain blue sweater she'd been wearing and pulled on the sweatshirt, added a pair of Christmas ball earrings and gave her hair a quick brush. She was ready.

She bounced down the front stairs, sending up a quick plea to the Spirit of Christmas Present: Please let my cookie exchange be a success.

CHAPTER THREE

Still 16 days 'til Xmas

Of course it would be a success, she thought, smoothing her sweatshirt nervously as she checked the living room and dining room one last time. The holiday decorations were festive, and Bill had even laid a fire for her in the living room fireplace. She took one of the long fireplace matches out of its box and lit it, bending down to set the fire alight. Then she lit the candles on the mantelpiece and on the sideboard, and switched off the brightest lamps. Studying the effect, she nodded in satisfaction. In candlelight, the odd stains and worn spots disappeared, and the rooms looked quite lovely.

She only saw two storm clouds on the horizon: Lee Cummings's separation and Richie's acceptance at Harvard. But thanks to Sue, she knew all about Lee's tendency to monopolize the conversation with her separation. If that happened, resolved Lucy, she would just have to change the subject, firmly. The cookie exchange wasn't a group-therapy session, no matter what Lee might think. And Sue would help out, too. In fact, she'd promised to come early.

As for the matter of Richie, well, Lucy suspected that his early acceptance at Harvard might have put quite a few maternal noses out of joint. Andrea Rogers was particularly competitive; she had been ever since Toby and Richie and the other boys had all been on the same Little League team. Thank goodness Marge had said she was coming, having completed her first round of chemotherapy. She was so down-to-earth and unpretentious, and could be counted on to express her genuine happiness for Richie's success to his mother, Rachel. With Marge on hand the natural competitiveness of the group would be kept in check.

Pushing open the kitchen door, Lucy saw that Sara was almost finished wiping the counters.

"Thanks, sweetheart," she said. "You did a really good job."

"No problem, Mom. Oh, Elizabeth said to tell you that the upstairs toilet is clogged up again."

"Oh, no. That's all I need tonight."

"Want me to tell Dad to fix it?"

"No. Not now." Lucy knew that Bill's plumbing projects tended to get very messy indeed. "He'll have to take it apart, and that means turning off the water. Listen, just do me a favor and ask everybody to use the downstairs toilet, okay?"

"Do we have to? I hate having to be polite and talking to your friends. Mrs. Orenstein always wants to know what books I've been reading and Ms. Small pinches my cheeks."

"Use the back stairs. You won't have to talk to them then."

"Okay, Mom."

The doorbell rang just as Sara disappeared up the stairs and Lucy looked at her watch. Only six-fifty. It was probably Sue, keeping her promise to come early to help out. But when Lucy opened the door she recognized Stephanie Scott, one of the young mothers from the day-care center Sue had suggested inviting.

"Hi, Steffie. You're the first. Come on in."

"I hope you don't mind that I came a little early," said Steffie, carefully maneuvering her tray of cookies through the door. "Tom — that's my husband — he asked me to bring some MADD pamphlets. But I wanted to make sure it was OK with you, so I thought I'd better get here before everybody else."

"Mad pamphlets?" asked a puzzled Lucy, taking the cookies and leading the way to the dining room. She lifted the foil and peeked, nodding with satisfaction at what looked like old-fashioned mincemeat cookies.

"Right," said Steffie, with a nod that made her perky short blond hair bounce. "Mothers Against Drunk Driving. They have a campaign this time every year to cut down on holiday accidents."

"These look yummy," said Lucy, setting the cookies down on the table.

"Just an old family recipe, they're quick and easy," said Steffie, slipping out of her coat and handing it to Lucy. She began digging in her enormous leather shoulder bag. "Now, about the pamphlets — I thought we could just put them out next to the cookies."

Lucy regarded the handful of brochures doubtfully. "I don't think . . ."

"Oh, but nobody could object, could they?" asked Steffie earnestly. "After all, we're all mothers, and this is from *Mothers* Against Drunk Driving. And Tom, that's my husband, tells me they are doing an absolutely fabulous job. He's a police lieutenant, and he has the utmost respect for MADD. He says they're one organization that is really making a difference."

Steffie's blue eyes were blazing and she was speaking with all the zeal of a true convert. Lucy felt a little prickle of resentment. This was her party, after all. Steffie had no business promoting her agenda in Lucy's house.

"It's certainly a worthy cause . . ." began Lucy, intending to firmly reject Steffie's offer, but realizing in mid-sentence that there was no way she could decently refuse. She could hardly argue in favor of drunk driving. What was she going to say that wouldn't sound irresponsible? She realized she was trapped, and began to think she really didn't like Steffie all that much.

The phone rang just then, and Lucy seized on the opportunity to avoid the issue. "Fine," she said, with a dismissive wave of the hand, reaching for the receiver.

"Lucy, this is Marge."

Oh, no, thought Lucy, watching as Steffie began arranging her pamphlets on the table. She can't come.

"Hi. How are you doing?"

"Not so good — that's why I'm calling." Marge spoke slowly, as if even talking on the phone was an effort. "I'm sorry, but I just can't make it tonight."

Lucy had known this might happen, but she was still disappointed.

"That's too bad . . ." she began, passing the coat back to Steffie and pointing her to the coat closet.

"I know. I was really hoping I could come. I got the candy-cane cookies all made, and Sue's going to pick 'em up and bring 'em. But I guess making the cookies used up all my energy. I'm beat now."

Lucy hoped it was the effects of the chemotherapy that was making Marge feel bad, and not the cancer, but she didn't know how to ask.

"I heard you're having a rough time with the chemo."

"You can say that again. If I can just survive the treatment, I'll have this thing licked," she said, with a weak chuckle. "At least, that's what they tell me."

"You hang in there," said Lucy. She thought of Marge's husband, Police Officer Barney Culpepper, and her son, Eddie, who was Toby's age. "Barney and Eddie need you."

"I know they do," replied Marge, with a little catch in her voice. "They've been terrific, you know. Hardly let me do a thing in the house. They keep saying I've got to save my energy to fight the cancer."

"They're right. You concentrate on getting well. I'll make sure you get your cookies. I'll bring them over one day this week."

"That'll be great. Thanks, Lucy."

What rotten luck, thought Lucy, slowly replacing the receiver. Marge was barely forty and the rumors around town were that her prognosis wasn't good, but she was fighting with every ounce of strength she had.

That's all you can do, thought Lucy, who feared every month when she examined her breasts that she'd find a lump.

"That was Marge Culpepper," Lucy told Steffie by way of explanation. "Her husband is on the police force, too."

"I think I've heard Tom mention his name."

"Well, Marge can't come tonight. She's been having chemotherapy and doesn't feel very well."

"Cancer?"

Lucy nodded. "I have a few things to do in the kitchen, so why don't you make yourself comfortable? I'll be right back."

She hurried into the kitchen, where she set up the coffeepot and filled the kettle with water for tea. Then she filled the sugar bowl and creamer and carried them out to the dining room, setting them on the side-board along with the cake. Turning toward the living room, where Steffie was perched on the couch and leafing through a coffee-table book, Lucy thought it was about time for Sue to show up. After all, Steffie was her friend.

As if by magic, the doorbell rang just then.

"Come on in," cried Lucy, welcoming reinforcements in the form of Juanita Oren-stein and Rachel Goodman. Juanita's little girl, Sadie, was Zoe's best friend.

"Before I forget — congratulations, Rachel. Toby told me all about Richie."

"Thanks, Lucy," said Rachel, glowing with maternal pride. "I can still hardly believe it myself, and I was the one who encouraged him to give Harvard a try."

"You never know unless you try," added Juanita, sagely.

"What? What's happened?" asked Steffie, joining the group in the hallway.

"Oh, where are my manners?" Lucy rolled her eyes. "Let me introduce Steffie Scott. This is Rachel Goodman — her son was just accepted at Harvard — and . . ."

"Harvard!" shrieked Steffie, sounding like one of the hysterical winners in a Publishers Clearinghouse commercial. "That's fantastic!"

Lucy and Juanita's eyes met. Lucy raised her eyebrows, and Juanita gave a little smirk.

"Actually," said Rachel, whose glow of pride had been replaced with a blush of embarrassment, "the best part is having the whole application process over with. I'm so glad he decided to try for early decision — now he doesn't have to worry and can enjoy his senior year."

"Well, I've been reading up on this," said Steffie. "My son, Will, is only three, but it's never too early to start planning. And the experts say that early decision definitely increases your chances at the top schools."

"Does it really? I didn't know that," said Rachel. "Actually, Richie's grandfather went to Harvard, and I think that had more to do with his admission than anything else."

"Really?" asked Steffie, her eyes round in surprise. "I didn't know they took Jews way back then."

For a moment the women stood in shocked silence. Then Rachel spoke. "You're probably right, though I'm sure it's nothing they're proud of today. And anyway, it was my dad who went, and he's not Jewish. My maiden name is Webster. For the record, Bob's folks are Jewish, but I have to confess we don't really practice any religion at all." She chuckled. "On Sunday mornings we walk the dog and read the paper."

"I didn't mean to give the wrong impression," said Steffie, realizing she'd made a blunder. "It doesn't matter to me what religion you are. Can I help you with those cookies?"

Hearing a knock, Lucy opened the door. As she suspected, it was Franny, who preferred a quiet rap to the gong of the doorbell.

"It's just me and Lydia," she said, with a nod toward her friend, kindergarten teacher Lydia Volpe. "I hope I parked OK. I didn't want to block anybody in." She was looking anxiously over her shoulder.

"She's parked fine," said Lydia, with a shrug. "I kept telling her."

"I'm sure it's fine. Let me take that," said Lucy, reaching for the cookie tin Franny was clutching to her bosom.

"Just the same old Chinese noodle cookies — I'm not much of a cook and you don't have to bake them. You just melt the chocolate and add the noodles and peanuts and drop them on waxed paper. I could never make pizzelles like Lydia — I don't know how she does it. They seem so difficult."

"Not really," said Lydia. "Trust me. I'm not really a good cook — not like my mother."

"Well, I'm sure they're both delicious. As always. My kids love them. It wouldn't be Christmas without them."

"You're sweet to say so, Lucy," said Franny, idly picking up one of the pamphlets.

"If we brought mudpies, Lucy would find something nice to say," joked Lydia.

"Don't the cookies look good this year? Don't tell me you made this cake, Lucy. It looks delicious," said Franny.

"Mmm, it does," agreed Lydia. "Now what can we do to help?"

Lucy looked up as the door flew open and Pam Stillings and Andrea Rogers sailed in.

"Would you be dears and bring in the coffee? The pot's in the kitchen. And the tea water ought to be ready, too."

"Be glad to," said Lydia, as she and Franny headed for the kitchen.

Lucy went to greet the new arrivals.

"We didn't ring the bell — we figured you'd have your hands full," announced Pam, who was married to Lucy's boss at *The Pennysaver,* Ted Stillings.

"Well, come on in and make yourselves at home. You know where everything is."

"I made my usual decorated sugar cookies," said Andrea, handing a basket to Lucy. Her eyes were bright, and her color was high. Lucy wondered if she had a fever.

"Are you feeling OK?" she asked in a concerned voice.

"Who me? I'm fine," said Andrea, avoiding Lucy's eyes and looking around the hallway to the rooms beyond. "Doesn't everything look wonderful? I'm so glad you decided to continue the cookie exchange. It's such a wonderful tradition."

"How many years, Lucy?" inquired Pam.

"It must be sixteen, anyway," guessed Lucy.

"That's right. I think Adam was still in diapers when I came for the first time."

"And Tim hadn't even begun playing baseball, yet," said Andrea, who always thought of her son's growth in terms of his progress in the sport. "Remember Little League? Wasn't that fun?"

"It sure was," said Lucy, winking at Pam. Their sons hadn't shown much talent for baseball, and they mostly remembered the games as opportunities for the boys to make humiliating mistakes. Andrea, however, had afforded everyone a great deal of amusement as a one-woman cheering section for Tim.

"I always knew baseball would pay off for Tim," continued Andrea. "And it has. You know quite a few scouts were interested in him last season, and we got a call from the athletic director at Maine Christian University this afternoon." Andrea's voice was rising and had become quite loud. "He got a full scholarship — tuition, room and board, even a little spending money. Isn't that fantastic?"

"Congratulations! That's great news," said Lydia, appearing in the doorway with the pot of coffee. "My little kindergarten grads are doing well. Did you hear about Richie?"

"What about Richie?" asked Andrea, narrowing her eyes suspiciously.

Here we go, thought Lucy.

"He's going to Harvard. Early decision," announced Lydia.

"No! That's great," said Pam, hurrying off to congratulate Rachel. "Good news for a change! Local boy does good!"

Andrea, of course, hadn't taken the news quite as well. To her way of thinking, Tim was tops. She didn't mind other kids being successful, she just didn't like them to outdo Tim. And while Maine Christian University was undoubtedly a fine school, it couldn't compare with Harvard.

"My that coffee smells good," said Andrea, with a little sniff. "I'd love a cup."

"You must be so proud of Tim," said Lucy, steering the conversation back to

Andrea's favorite subject. "He was on the All-State team last year, wasn't he?"

"And he won the batting title last year and was voted MVP by his teammates," recited Andrea, looking a little happier.

"He was always a little firecracker," said Lydia, who had long ago trained herself to remember only her students' positive attributes.

Confident she was leaving Andrea in good hands, Lucy left the group in the dining room and went into the living room to invite the women gathered there to take some refreshments.

"There's cake and coffee in the dining room — and I wouldn't dilly-dally," she said. "There's a pretty hungry crowd in there."

"I'm so glad you did this, Lucy. It's such a nice Christmas tradition," said Rachel, who was leaning back in a wing chair with her feet propped on a footstool. "But I can sure understand why Sue thought it was time to take a break. Is she coming?"

"I've been wondering the same thing," said Lucy. "She's supposed to, and she's bringing her new assistant at the center, Tucker."

"Tucker's wonderful," said Steffie, rising to her feet and joining the general drift toward the dining room. "Will just adores her."

As they passed through the hallway the doorbell rang and Lucy stopped to open it, expecting to see an apologetic Sue standing on the other side. Instead, she saw Lee Cummings.

"Just what I need," she muttered to herself. "The woman scorned, the soon-to-be divorcée from hell." She pasted a bright smile on her face. "Hi, Lee. I'm so glad you could make it."

"Me too, Lucy. For a while I didn't think I was going to be able to come. I was waiting for Steve, that weasel. I mean, to hear him talk he absolutely adores the girls, and I'm the evil witch who keeps him from them. But when it comes to taking care of them for one single evening, where is he? He forgot all about it. I had to call all over town, and I finally tracked him down at the donut shop." She paused for breath and shook her head. "I hope he chokes on them. I hope the cholesterol clogs up his blood vessels and he has a stroke and lies there paralyzed for days and nobody finds him until he rots. And when they find him the rats will have been chewing on him . . ."

"These cookies look really good," said Lucy, taking a platter covered with plastic wrap from her.

"It's the most wonderful recipe," said Lee, hanging up her jacket on the hall coat tree. "They taste great and believe it or not, they're low fat and have hardly any sugar. They're actually good for you."

Lucy raised a skeptical eyebrow. Lee took her role as the wife of a dentist very seriously, and was known for using recipes that were good for you but didn't necessarily taste very good.

"Sounds like a miracle."

"It really is — oh, Lucy, do you mind if I just run upstairs to use the loo?"

"Of course not," said Lucy, mentally crossing her fingers. So far, the plumbing seemed to be holding up but she didn't want to risk any disasters. "Please use the downstairs powder room instead. Do you know where it is?"

"Sure thing."

Lee dashed off through the kitchen, while Lucy added her platter of cookies to the others on the table. It was filling up, Lucy saw with satisfaction, surveying the array of homemade baked goods. The women had packed the cookies in sandwich bags, each holding six cookies, and a few had decorated them with bright holiday ribbons and stickers. The table was so crowded, in fact, that

Steffie's little brochures had disappeared from sight.

"So, what's it like to be the proud mother of a genius?" asked Lydia, striking up a conversation with Rachel. "You must be so proud of Richie."

"I am," admitted Rachel. "But I was proud of him before we got the letter, too."

"You don't have to be modest," said Lydia. "Harvard is the top American college, after all."

"There are plenty of other good schools, too," said Pam, who was growing tired of hearing about other people's kids. "Adam wants to go to Boston University, or maybe Northeastern."

"MCU's awfully good, too," said Andrea. "Especially if you have a full scholarship like Tim does."

"And a lot of kids can't take the pressure at a place like Harvard," continued Pam. "They crash and burn."

"That's right," added Steffie. "There's a lot of alcohol abuse at those fraternities. Was it Harvard? Maybe it was MIT. I'm not sure which, but I remember reading that a freshman died from alcohol poisoning."

"That was MIT," said Lee, joining the group. "But I don't think Harvard's much better. It certainly didn't do much for Steve,

I can tell you that."

There was a sudden commotion as Rachel dropped her coffee cup, shattering the cup and saucer and spilling the coffee on the rug. "Oh, I'm so sorry, Lucy," she said, dropping to her knees and attempting to clean up the mess with a holiday napkin.

"Here, let me take care of that," said Lucy. As she knelt beside Rachel, she saw that tears were filling her eyes. "It's nothing . . ." began Lucy, reaching for more napkins. "We spill stuff all the time — why do you think I'm having this little do by candlelight?"

Rachel giggled, and Lucy gave her a quick hug. She didn't think for a minute that Rachel was crying over spilt coffee; she had been upset by her friends' meanness.

"Don't pay any mind," whispered Lucy, taking the sponge Franny was offering her. "They're just jealous."

"Oh, I know. But I've really had to bite my tongue tonight, let me tell you. Especially with Andrea," hissed Rachel, picking up the broken pieces of china and handing them to Franny. "To listen to her, you'd never know Tim isn't quite the paragon she wants everyone to think he is."

"He isn't?" Lucy was definitely interested.

"No. He was arrested last week for driving under the influence. He's in big trouble."

"My goodness," said Franny.

"How do you know?" asked Lucy.

"They hired Bob to defend him." Bob, Rachel's husband, was a lawyer.

Rachel's hand flew to her mouth as she rose to her feet. "Don't tell anybody, okay? I'm not supposed to know about this — client confidentiality and all that."

"Your secret's safe with me," said Lucy, now standing and scanning the table for the brochures. She finally found them under Franny's Chinese noodle cookies. Making sure no one was watching, she lifted the plate and scooped up the brochures, wadding them into a ball along with the sodden napkins. Then she turned, intending to throw the whole mess into the kitchen garbage.

"Oh my goodness, Lucy," said Lee, suddenly appearing at her elbow. "Who brought those awful Chinese noodle cookies? Can you imagine making something as unhealthy as that in this day and age? What could she have been thinking? Those things are full of saturated fat and all sorts of preservatives. Talk about empty calories!"

Lucy looked across the table toward the sideboard, where Franny was refilling the teapot, and saw her hurt expression.

"Oh, I don't know," said Lucy, catching Franny's eye. "I can't resist them myself — and it's only once a year."

That's right, she told herself. Christmas only comes once a year, thank goodness. And with any luck, she'd never have to have this blasted cookie exchange again. How could she have forgotten? It was the same thing every year. Somebody always went home with hurt feelings. Of course, this year looked to be something of a record in the hurt-feelings department. It was all Sue's fault, she decided. If she'd gotten to the party on time, she could have helped keep the combatants apart. As it was, if she didn't arrive soon, thought Lucy, blood would probably be shed.

In the kitchen, Lucy tossed the pamphlets into the bin under the kitchen sink. The last thing she wanted was for Andrea to see them; remembering her swollen eyes when she arrived, Lucy was sure she was enormously upset about Tim's arrest. All that bragging about the MCU scholarship was her way of putting on a brave front.

Of course, nobody was more competitive than Andrea when it came to kids. As much as Lucy sympathized with her, and dreaded finding herself in the same situation, she couldn't help feeling just the teeniest bit that Andrea was getting her just deserts.

Lucy was far too superstitious ever to brag about her children; the most she would do was modestly accept a compliment on their behalf. That wasn't Andrea's way. Ever since Tim caught his first Wiffle ball, gently lobbed by his father, she had hailed him as a superb athlete. Her friends had listened patiently through the years as she had provided a play-by-play narration of his achievements. In his mother's eyes, Tim could do no wrong. He was perfect. He was, thought Lucy, too good to be true.

Returning to the dining room, Lucy poured herself a cup of coffee and propped a slice of cake on the saucer. Then she followed the group into the living room, where they had settled to enjoy their refreshments. Lee was making the most of this opportunity to reap her friends' sympathy by making sure they all knew the details of Steve's latest transgressions.

"He told his lawyer that there's no reason for me to get the stove because I never lifted a hand to cook a home-cooked meal in the entire seven years we've been married — can you believe it?"

Receiving clucks and murmurs of sympathy from the group, she continued. "I mean, we entertained at least once a week and I thought nothing of whipping up beef Stroganoff or coq au vin for his dental-society colleagues and their incredibly boring wives, not to mention chicken wings and home-made pizza — with sun-dried tomatoes, I might add — for his annual Super Bowl bash. This stuff didn't all just appear, you know. I spent hours cutting and chopping and stirring and sweating over a hot stove — the very stove he says I never touched. Can you believe it?"

"It's funny. If people don't do something themselves, they don't understand how much work it is," said Pam. "Ted doesn't have a clue about housework. I'm sure he thinks the rugs vacuum themselves while I lie on the couch all day watching soap operas."

The women chuckled and nodded in agreement.

"Don't even mention rugs," moaned Lee. "You know my beautiful Kirman, the one my parents gave us for a wedding present?"

"He wants that?" asked Lydia.

Lee nodded, and the women sighed and shook their heads in dismay.

"That's terrible," said Juanita.

"I'd tell him exactly what he could do with it," said Pam.

"Well, he's not going to get it," said Lee.

"I'm going to make sure of that. That's why I went with the Boston lawyer. He says he always goes right for the jugular!"

"And I bet he charges Boston prices, too," said Rachel, who was standing next to Lucy.

"Like the hair-dye commercial says, 'I'm worth it,' " said Lee, defending her choice. "Besides, I have my girls' futures to think of, too."

This was received with another murmur of approval, and Lee paused to take a bite of cake.

Rachel turned to Lucy. "She's making a big mistake," she whispered. "A local lawyer like Bob would try to get them to reconcile, or at least work out an amicable agreement. That would be a lot better for the kids, believe me."

Lucy nodded in agreement. She tended to think people were often too quick to opt for divorce and didn't consider the consequences, especially for the children. "I don't know — even if she gets everything she wants, she isn't going to be able to keep the same lifestyle. Whatever he makes, now it's got to support two households instead of one."

"That's right," said Rachel. "Except for a handful of very wealthy people, divorce is a one-way road to poverty."

"Yoo-hoo," halloed Sue, sailing through the front door. "Sorry I'm late . . ."

"It's about time you got here," complained Lucy, who had been wondering if Sue had abandoned her.

"Nice shirt — and so subtle, too," joked Sue, blinking at Lucy's bright Santa sweatshirt. "I would have been here hours ago except my battery died. So, how's it going?"

"Touch and go," said Lucy, with a little shrug. "No fatalities — yet."

"I'd say you're doing great," said Sue. Then, raising her voice, she announced, "Now, listen everybody. I know you can't wait to start grabbing cookies but I want you to meet someone. This is Tucker Whitney, my new assistant at the center."

Tucker, Lucy saw, could be trouble. She was a strikingly attractive twentysomething. Tall and slender, she had long, naturally blond hair.

"Hi, Tucker," chorused the group, without much enthusiasm. Realizing she was no longer the center of attention, Lee decided to pour herself a second cup of coffee.

"Hi, everybody," said Tucker, smiling broadly. Although she was the youngest person there and didn't know most of the others, she was one of those rare people who are comfortable wherever they go.

She turned to Lucy and indicated the stack of platters and tins in her arms. "What should I do with these? I hope I made enough. Sue didn't tell me how many to bring so I have these twelve dozen but if you need more, I've got another six dozen in the car."

"Oh, my goodness. You didn't need to do all that," said Lucy. "You only needed to bring six dozen."

"Oh, well, you can keep the extras," said Tucker. "Sue told me you've got four kids." She looked around at the house, obviously impressed. "You're so lucky. Someday I want to have a big family and a house just like this."

Lucy started to protest politely, but changed her mind. "You're right. I am lucky. Thanks for reminding me. Sometimes I take too much for granted."

"Don't we all," said Tucker. "Now, I hope everyone likes these cookies. It's a new recipe I got from a magazine, and it sounded too good to be true. They're supposed to be low in fat and sugar . . ."

"That can't be!" exclaimed Lee, glaring at Tucker from the other side of the table.

"Well, that's what it said," insisted Tucker.

"They're the same as my cookies!" Lee pointed an accusing finger at Tucker. "You stole my recipe!"

Tucker didn't reply, she just shrugged her shoulder apologetically.

Lucy felt a little bit like a firefighter, rushing to put out yet another flare of temper.

"It just goes to show that good recipes get around," she said. Out of the corner of her eye she saw Toby heading upstairs, looking like a young man with a mission, but before she could remind him to use the downstairs bathroom she was distracted by Tucker's request to borrow something to put her cookies in.

"I didn't think to bring an extra container," she confessed.

"Not a problem," said Lucy, pulling a bread basket out of the sideboard and giving it to her. "Don't mind Lee," she added. "She's involved in a messy divorce."

"I know. Her little girl, Hillary, comes to the day-care center. She talks about it a lot. She's pretty upset about Daddy leaving home."

"That's too bad," responded Lucy automatically, her attention drawn to the living room.

There, as if in slow motion, she saw Franny approaching Andrea, holding out something. Oh my God, she thought, realizing that Franny, dear, well-meaning

Franny, had saved one of the MADD pamphlets and was intending to give it to Andrea. No doubt expecting her to be grateful for this show of concern.

Lucy immediately started across the room, hoping to intercept Franny before the exchange could take place. In her haste, her foot slipped out of her loafer and she began to fall. She caught herself by grabbing the doorjamb and quickly shoved her foot back into the shoe.

"What is this? A joke?" exclaimed Andrea, glaring at Franny.

Lucy hurried to explain. "Steffie brought these pamphlets. Her husband is . . ."

"I know exactly who her husband is," hissed Andrea.

"Well, if I'd known about Tim, I never would have let her put the pamphlets out. And as soon as I heard, I threw them away. I'm sure Franny was only trying to be helpful."

"That's right," sniffed Franny.

To Lucy's dismay, Steffie joined their little group and placed her hand on Andrea's arm.

"It's very normal to feel angry about Tim's arrest, but it's for his own good," she said. "My husband has seen too many terrible accidents where kids, kids like Tim,

61

have been killed. Isn't it better for him to learn that drinking and driving is unacceptable? I mean," she continued with the bright certainty of the mother of a blameless three-year-old, "I would much rather spend a morning in court with Will than a night in the emergency room."

"Well, I wouldn't be so confident, if I were you," said Andrea, pulling her arm free of Steffie's grasp. Her voice rang out shrilly, and the other women dropped their conversations and turned toward her.

"I know what you're thinking, all of you," continued Andrea, her eyes flashing with anger. "You're all positive that something like this will never happen to you because you're good mothers. It's only bad mothers whose kids get in trouble. And you've done everything right. You've cooked dinner every night. OK, so once in a while you order pizza, but that's as bad as it gets. Right?"

Pam and Juanita chuckled nervously.

"You don't let the kids watch too much TV — it's not good for them. And you don't let them eat too many sweets because you want them to have strong teeth. You go to church every Sunday, and you make sure the kids go to Sunday School."

Franny dabbed at her eyes, which were filling with tears.

"Most of all, you've been good examples. You don't drink and drive, and your kids would never dream of doing it. Oh, no. You've spoken with them and told them that if they need a ride home, they should call you. No matter what the time. You'll get them, no questions asked. Right?"

A few heads around the room nodded, including Lucy's. She and Bill had had that very talk with Toby just a few weeks ago.

"Well, you know what?" demanded Andrea, who was shaking with rage and shame. "I am a good mother. I've done all those things. And my son was arrested. The lawyer tells me he'll have a criminal record for the rest of his life. So don't be so sure it can't happen to you."

Stunned, the women were silent, staring at Andrea, who was wiping tears from her face. Nobody seemed to know what to say. Realizing she had a social disaster on her hands, Lucy hurried to Andrea, proffering a napkin printed with holly. She gave her a little hug and turned to face the group.

"Come on, everybody. It's time to swap those cookies. Remember, you can only take a half dozen of each kind. Okay?"

The women picked up the empty baskets and cookie tins they had brought and formed a loose line that wrapped around the table. Only Andrea remained in the living room, being consoled by Tucker.

"Have you ever seen anything like this?" cooed Juanita. "The cookies this year are better than ever."

"They're absolutely wonderful," agreed Pam.

"I don't know how I'm going to keep them hidden until Christmas Eve," confessed Lucy. From upstairs, she thought she heard the sound of the toilet flushing. Then she remembered Toby, hurrying upstairs with an especially purposeful expression. She held her breath, willing the aged pipes to cooperate, just this once.

"We have ours on Christmas Day with hot cocoa," said Pam, counting six Chinese noodle cookies into a sandwich bag.

"I take mine to my folks' house," said Lee. "We always have Christmas with them."

Lucy reached across the table to take some of Tucker's cookies when she felt a drop of water on her hand. She looked up and, horrified, saw the dining-room ceiling beginning to sag, the plaster bulging with water.

"I felt a drop," said Lee. "Lucy, I think you have a leak . . ."

Lucy was standing openmouthed, transfixed by the sight of the bulging plaster bubble growing even larger.

"Quick! Pick up the table!" ordered Sue, taking in the situation. "We can carry it . . ."

The women hurried to obey, struggling to lift the solid mahogany table Bill and Lucy had bought at an estate sale. But as Lucy watched, the drops of water began coming faster and faster, rapidly forming a trickle that in only a few moments more became a stream. Finally, just as the women were beginning to shift the heavy table, the plaster let go. It fell on the cookie-covered table with a thump, followed by a deluge of water that poured onto the table and then cascaded onto the floor, splashing everyone.

"Wow," said Sue, wrapping an arm around Lucy's shoulder and giving her a squeeze. "You sure know how to give one heck of a party."

CHAPTER FOUR

15 days 'til Christmas

Wednesday morning, it took every bit of Lucy's willpower to drag herself out of bed. All she wanted to do was to pull the covers over her head and forget everything — especially the cookie exchange.

Once the flooding started, time had seemed to switch to slow motion. She remembered the horrified faces, and the polite assurances that "it didn't matter one bit, we had a wonderful time, anyway" as the women departed, leaving her to face the sodden mess. Franny had offered to help clean up, but Lucy had sent her on her way, preferring to handle it herself.

Bill had helped, holding a big trash bag open for her so she could dump the ruined cookies into it. It almost made her cry, thinking of all the work the soggy cookies represented, all those expensive ingredients gone to waste.

She groaned, turning over and burying her face in her pillow.

"You've got to get up," said Bill, nibbling on her ear.

"I don't want to."

"Tough," said Bill, whacking her bottom with a pillow.

Lucy didn't get up, she burrowed deeper under the covers, but she knew she was just postponing the inevitable. Bill was right. She had to get up. She had to get the lunches made and the kids off to school, then, she had to go straight to *The Pennysaver* and write up the selectmen's meeting in time for the noon deadline. Ted was counting on her. She rolled over and got out of bed.

"Thanks, Lucy, you did a real nice job with this," said Ted, after he had given the story a quick edit. He scratched his chin and smiled slyly. "I guess the real story was your cookie exchange. Pam said you had quite a flood."

"Don't remind me," said Lucy, buttoning up her coat. "I've never been so embarrassed in my life."

"These things happen to everyone," said Ted. "Don't forget the kindergarten Christmas party on Monday, okay?"

"I'll have it for you Tuesday," promised Lucy.

She took his nod as a dismissal and left the office, scowling at the cheery jangle of the bell on the door. Crossing Main Street to her parked car, she consulted her mental list of things to do. She could pick up a few presents, she could tackle the Christmas cards, she could get started on Zoe's angel costume for the Christmas pageant . . . the list went on and on.

Nope, she decided, shifting the list to a mental "do later" file. Right now, she needed some tea and sympathy. She climbed in the car and started the engine, driving down the street to the rec building.

Sue's reaction, when she looked up from the sand table where she was helping two little boys build a racetrack for their Matchbox cars, was not what Lucy had hoped for.

"That was some party last night," said Sue, giggling. "If you could have seen the look on your face when the water started dripping — I never saw anything so funny in my life."

"Well, I'm glad somebody had a good time." Lucy plopped herself down in a child-sized chair. She glanced around the room, where another boy was busy building a tower of blocks and a group of little girls were playing in the dress-up area, and asked, "Where's your helper?"

Sue shrugged her shoulders. "No phone call, no nothing. It's a heck of an inconvenience. I had to call the moms of the three infants and have them make other arrangements. You know, I really thought Tucker was different. Mature. Responsible." She shook her head. "Sooner or later, they all revert to form. She's only a kid, after all. I don't know what I was thinking."

"I don't know. I was pretty impressed with her. She was the life of the party, until the party . . ."

"Died a watery death?"

"It needed to be put out of its misery, believe me."

Lucy watched as Sue put an arm around one of the little boys and began gently stroking his stomach.

"Take it easy, Will," she coaxed. "Just relax."

Will's narrow chest, however, continued to rise and fall rapidly under his OshKosh overalls.

"Is that Steffie's Will?" Lucy asked, putting two and two together.

"Yup. This is my friend, Will, and this is Harry," said Sue. "Boys, this is Mrs. Stone."

"Glad to meet you," said Lucy, reaching across the table and shaking their hands. Harry smiled brightly at her, but Will, intent on his struggle to breathe, only gave her a glance.

Sue pulled an inhaler out of her pocket and he obediently took a puff, and then another.

Lucy glanced at Will, raised her eyebrows, then shifted her gaze to Sue. "You know it was Steffie who brought the MADD pamphlets. I got rid of them as soon as I heard about Tim, but Franny must have saved one. I know her intentions were good, but Andrea didn't see it that way."

"That woman" — Sue tipped her head toward Will — "must be a fanatic. Why would you bring something like that to a party? I mean, you could very well have served wine. That would've put the kibosh on things."

"It really threw me when she showed up with the darn things. I didn't know what to do."

"I don't know what else you could have done, under the circumstances." Sue pushed a little red car along in the sand, following the road Harry was making with his toy bulldozer. "And to tell the truth, I feel badly for Andrea, but Tim's gotta learn, too. This

70

isn't the first time he's been driving drunk; it's just the first time he got caught."

Lucy nodded thoughtfully, watching Will. He looked as if he could use another puff on the inhaler, but she knew it was too soon. Elizabeth had asthma, and Lucy had often helped her manage an attack.

"Lee didn't help matters much, either," said Lucy. "You were right about her. All she can talk about is how badly Steve's behaving. And what was that about Tucker stealing her cookie recipe?" Lucy looked puzzled. "I didn't understand that at all."

Sue snorted. "She isn't worried about her cookie recipe, believe me. She's afraid Tucker is stealing her husband." Sue paused, and put a comforting arm around Will's shoulder. The little boy's eyes looked huge under his bangs. "Steve's been dating Tucker. She told me all about it last night."

"Ohhh," said Lucy, "now it makes sense." She reached across the table and gently pinched Will's chin, but he didn't look at her. He was entirely focused on his struggle to breathe and was beginning to panic. "I don't like the look of this," said Lucy. "I think he needs a nebulizer."

Sue nodded. "Can you stay here, until I get back?"

"No problem." Lucy noticed Will's eyes

were beginning to roll up into his head. "You better hurry. Get your coat." She picked up Will and carried him over to the cubby area, where the coats were kept, and began zipping him into his jacket.

Sue grabbed her coat and yanked open a desk drawer, pulling out Will's emergency file. She took out a card and tucked the manila folder under her arm.

"Notify his folks, okay?" she told Lucy, handing her the card. "They can meet me at the emergency room." Then she scooped up the little boy and hurried off.

Lucy took a quick head count on the remaining kids. Harry, she saw, had gone to join the little boy who was playing with blocks. Two of the girls had moved into the toy kitchen, and Hillary Cummings was piling stuffed toys into a doll carriage. Everything seemed under control, so she sat down at Sue's desk to phone Steffie.

Looking at the number printed on the card, Lucy hesitated and let her fingers play with the numbered buttons on the keypad. After last night, she didn't really want to talk to Steffie. Her conscience took over, however, before she could decide if her reluctance was due to anger with Steffie or embarrassment over the leak, and she punched in the number.

Listening to the phone ring, she thought about the frail little boy Steffie seemed to have such high hopes for. Finally, the phone was answered; it turned out to be a bank in the next town, Gilead, and she was connected to Steffie.

"Of course. You couldn't call my husband," sighed Steffie, when Lucy explained the situation.

"I didn't think of that," said Lucy, remembering the police station was just around the corner. She flipped over the card. "Actually, yours is the only number we have."

"I can't believe this," fumed Steffie. "As it happens, I'm in a very important meeting, and I can't leave right now. I'm sure Will's in good hands at the cottage hospital."

"Do you want me to try your husband?" asked Lucy, somewhat stunned. She couldn't imagine reacting as Steffie had, but then, she hadn't tried to juggle a demanding career with motherhood.

"Never mind," snapped Steffie. "I'll get there as soon as I can, but I'm at least ten miles away."

Well, thought Lucy, replacing the receiver, at least Will is with Sue and she won't leave until his mother shows up.

Realizing it might be a while before Sue returned, Lucy went around the room, chatting with each of the children. She suspected they might be concerned about Sue's sudden departure, and she wanted to introduce herself and let them know that she would be taking care of them. Then she spotted a tray with a pitcher and a plate of cookies, and realized it was well past snack time.

As soon as she placed the tray on the table, the children came running and jostled for seats.

"Wow, you guys must be hungry," said Lucy, pouring cups of apple juice for them. "There's plenty for everyone."

She sat down with them and played a name game. The first child said his name, Justin, and the second child had to say Justin's name and add hers, Hillary. The third child, Emily, had to say the other names in order: Justin, Hillary, Emily.

Lucy was last, and she pretended to have a terrible time remembering all the names. The kids thought she was hilarious, and had a rollicking good time laughing at a stupid grown-up. Finally, when everyone had finished their snack, she recited the names in proper order and sent the kids over to the cubbies to put on their jackets so they could all go out for some fresh air. While they did that, she cleared up the snack things and gave the table a quick wipe.

By the time she joined them, the kids had done a pretty good job with their coats. She knelt down and helped them with zippers and buttons, and made sure they had their mittens on. Then she slipped into her own coat and led the little line over to the door. She was just about to open it, when Officer Barney Culpepper's face appeared in the glass window.

"Hi, Officer Culpepper," she said, opening the door. "What can we do for you today?" She assumed he was there for one of the many safety programs he presented at local schools — maybe bike safety, or stranger danger. So did the kids, who clustered around him, demanding to see his walkie-talkie. But today Officer Culpepper wasn't smiling, his St. Bernard jowls were drooping and he looked very grim.

"Go on outside, children. It's playtime," said Lucy. "Officer Culpepper will be back another day."

"What's the matter?" asked Lucy, fearing that his wife, Marge, had taken a turn for the worse.

"Where's Sue?" Barney looked through the doorway. "I need to talk to her."

"At the hospital. Will Scott had an asthma attack. Can I help you?"

"Maybe." Barney took off his blue cap and

scratched his brush cut. "I probably shouldn't tell you but, heck, it's gonna be all over town soon enough, anyway." He held the cap in his hands and shifted his weight from one foot to the other. Finally, he spoke. "Tucker Whitney was killed this morning. A neighbor noticed her front door was open and called 911. The responding officer found her dead, inside the house."

Lucy collapsed against the doorframe, feeling as if she'd been punched in the stomach. "I can't believe it. I just saw her last night."

"It's terrible." Barney shook his head.

Lucy's mind was in a whirl, trying to understand how a healthy young girl like Tucker could be dead. "Was it an accident?"

"Doesn't look like it. They're not saying anything until the medical examiner is through, but it sure looks like murder."

"How?" Lucy asked in a small voice.

"She was strangled. At least that's what they think."

"Oh my God." Lucy closed her eyes and leaned against the doorjamb. Then, hearing a shriek from the play yard, she was reminded of her responsibilities.

"Justin, Matthew — one at a time on the slide, please," she said, struggling to keep her voice level.

She looked up at Barney, blinking back tears. "I just can't believe it. Who would do such a thing?"

Barney shook his head sadly. "It's early, still. I don't know if they have any suspects, yet. I came to see if she had an address book or anything like that here — they didn't find anything at her place."

"I don't know. I think she used the desk by the window. You can look around."

"Thanks, Lucy. I'll be out of your way in a minute."

"No problem."

Shoving her hands in her pockets, Lucy strolled out to the play area. It wasn't too cold, maybe thirty-five degrees, and it was bright and sunny, but Lucy felt chilled to the bone. The kids didn't seem to mind the cold one bit. The boys were scrambling up the ladder and shrieking as they went down the slide, a couple of the girls were bouncing on plastic horses fastened to sturdy springs. Two others were going up and down on the seesaw. It all seemed so normal. A typical day at the day-care center. Maybe it was, she thought, finding comfort in denial. Maybe she'd imagined the whole thing. Barney hadn't come, and Tucker was still alive.

"Thanks, Lucy," came Barney's voice, from over the fence. She turned and saw him, tipping his hat at her. "I'll be on my way now."

She lifted her hand to wave and a dark wave of grief overwhelmed her, like clouds rolling in and blotting out the sun. She sat down on a bench and watched the children play, but they seemed very far away, and their voices were muffled. It was only when she heard the steeple bell at the community church tolling the noon hour that she realized it was time to go inside for lunch. Otherwise, she didn't know how long she might have sat there.

CHAPTER FIVE

To the children, the bells meant it was lunchtime. Shrieking, they ran for the door and tumbled inside.

But to Lucy, they sounded like funeral bells, tolling the years of a life that was far too brief. Distracted, she went through the motions automatically, helping the children hang up their coats in the cubbies and telling them to wash their hands. Used to the routine, they were soon sitting at the table, waiting for Lucy to get their lunches out of the refrigerator and bring them to the table.

They thought it was hysterical when she gave Justin's blue lunch box to Harry; everyone knew Harry had a Power Ranger lunch box. Their laughter roused Lucy, and she reluctantly returned to the here and now, letting go of Tucker's death for the time being.

"Are you sure the Power Ranger lunch box is Harry's?" she teased, peeking inside.

"I see Oreos — I think it must be mine."

All the children laughed, except Harry, who appeared a bit anxious.

"Oops, I forgot," said Lucy, slapping her hand to her head. "I didn't bring any lunch today. This must be Harry's!"

With a big sigh of relief Harry took the box and opened it up. Like the other children he began arranging the contents on the table in front of him.

Lucy went into the kitchen to get the milk and grabbed a few graham crackers for herself. After she poured the milk she sat with the children, nibbling on the crackers. She noticed that they all followed the same pattern: first they ate their cookies and fruit, after a lively trading session in which one fruit roll-up went for a box of raisins and two Vienna fingers, then they took a bite or two out of their sandwiches and discarded the rest.

Lucy was tidying the table, sighing over the waste, when Sue returned without Will.

"They wanted to keep him for a while, to make sure he isn't coming down with something, and I was afraid I'd never get away," complained Sue, "but his mother finally showed up. She had to cancel 'two very important meetings, mind you.' " Sue was a good mimic, and copied Steffie's officious tone perfectly. Lucy almost smiled.

"Hey, what's the matter?" prompted Sue. "You look as if something awful's happened."

"Barney came by with some bad news," began Lucy, wishing there was some way to soften what she had to say. "Tucker's dead."

"What?" Sue didn't believe what she heard.

"It's true. She was found dead this morning. A neighbor noticed the front door was open and called the police. Barney came here looking for an address book, so they can notify her family."

"Was it an accident?" Sue was struggling to understand.

Lucy shook her head. "They think she was strangled," she said, her voice breaking.

"Oh my God." Sue collapsed on a little chair, her long, elegant legs splayed out at an awkward angle.

Noticing the increase in the volume of the children's voices, Lucy turned her attention to them. Two of the girls were fighting over the bride's veil in the dress-up corner and Justin and Matthew were crashing toy wooden cars into each other.

"Okay, quiet down," she said, rising to her feet and giving Sue's hand a little pat. "It's time for a story."

Back in the familiar groove of their daily routine, the children gathered on the rug in the corner and sat cross-legged. Lucy settled herself in the rocking chair and opened the first book that came to hand. Afterward, she couldn't have said what book it was, but it held the kids' attention. Then, knowing the drill, they unrolled their mats and settled down for quiet time. Lucy popped a cassette of soothing music into the tape recorder and went back to Sue.

"Can I get you some tea? Something to eat?"

Sue didn't respond, so Lucy put two mugs of water in the microwave to heat and raided the graham-cracker box once again. Hearing the ding, she dropped tea bags into the mugs.

"Drink this," she urged Sue.

Sue took the mug with shaking hands. "I just can't believe this. I was with her yesterday."

"I know." Lucy sipped her tea. "You know what I was thinking last night, when I was talking to Tucker? I was thinking how wonderful it would be to be young again and have my whole life ahead of me."

Sue shook her head. "It's not fair. She loved life — she had so much enthusiasm. Once I asked her if she didn't get depressed sometimes, and you know what she said? She said she woke up every morning convinced that the day held something wonderful for her, and it was up to her to find that beautiful thing. It might be a smile from one of the kids, or a postcard from a friend, or a kitten . . ." Sue's face crumpled as she dissolved into tears.

Lucy wrapped an arm around Sue's shoulder and let her cry, grateful they were hidden from the children's view by a bookcase. Raffi's gentle voice drifted across the room. Finally, Sue's shoulders stopped heaving, and she wiped her eyes with a tissue.

"I'm sorry, Lucy. I don't know what's the matter with me. It must be the shock."

"You don't need to apologize. You have a right to grieve." Lucy wondered who else would be grieving for Tucker and remembered Barney's visit. "You know, Barney was looking for an address book but I don't think he found anything."

"She had a bright pink agenda — you know, calendar, address book, your whole life wrapped up with a Velcro flap." Sue sniffled and reached for another tissue.

"How big was it?" asked Lucy, going over to Tucker's desk. The top was bare except for a plant, a small pink mitten, and a picture of a smiling middle-aged couple.

83

Lucy picked it up for a closer look. Tucker had inherited her coloring from her mother, but her smile came from her dad.

"About like this." Sue described a ten-inch square with her hands. "It was chunky, a couple of inches thick."

"It wouldn't fit in a pocket?" Lucy replaced the picture and slid the center drawer open. It was empty, except for a clutter of pens and pencils in the tray designed for them. Pulling open the top drawer on the side, Lucy noticed Sue had joined her.

"No, it was pretty big." Sue peered in the drawer. "She'd only been here a few months. She didn't have time to accumulate much."

The drawer held only a bottle of Advil and a spare pair of panty hose.

"What brought her here?" asked Lucy, pulling open the middle drawer and lifting out a sweater.

"She'd finished two years of college and wanted a break. Her folks said OK, as long as she did something useful. I almost fainted when she walked in one day, answering the help-wanted ad. I never expected to get anyone with her qualifications, not for what we pay. But she said she didn't need much money, she was living in her parents' summer house on the coast road."

Lucy raised an eyebrow. Smith Heights

Road overlooked the cove and was lined with enormous, gray-shingled "cottages" belonging to wealthy old-line families who summered in Tinker's Cove but lived in New York, Washington, or Philadelphia. Among them were a cabinet secretary, a prominent pediatrician whose name had become a household word, and the celebrated talk-show hostess, Norah Hemmings. Others were CEOs or lawyers or investment bankers.

In the bottom drawer Lucy found a well-worn pair of loafers, a handful of college catalogs, and a guide to hiking trails.

Sue picked up one of the catalogs and fanned the pages. "She was thinking of changing her major — she wanted to concentrate in early childhood education. I warned her it was a bad career move — low-paying, not respected — but she said she didn't care. She said she loved working with kids." Sue closed her eyes and took a deep, quavery breath. "She said she'd never been happier."

Sue bent down to replace the catalogs in the drawer and gently shut it. When she stood up, her eyes were glistening.

"No sign of the agenda, here. And I know Barney didn't take it. I would've noticed."

"She usually carried a gym bag. She took

a tai chi class after work. That's probably where it is. We don't need it, anyway. I have next-of-kin information on her emergency card." She sighed. "I can't let them nap forever. I've got to get them up. Would you call the police station for me?"

Lucy nodded. Sue stood up, then sat down, propping her elbow on the desk and resting her head in her hand. "Damn — I've got to find someone to replace Tucker." She rubbed her eyes. "At Christmastime, no less."

"Don't panic. I can help out some. And I bet there are plenty of young moms who could use some extra Christmas cash."

"We'll see." Sue didn't seem convinced. She got back up and, walking slowly, went over to the bookcase and clicked off the tape recorder, reaching her hands high over her head. "C'mon kids. It's time to get up — let's see you all give a big stretch."

While Sue led the children in their wake-up exercises, Lucy went to the phone and dialed the police station, asking for Barney.

"Did you find what you were looking for?" she asked.

"Nope. Not a thing."

"Sue says she had a pink agenda, one of those organizer books, and she kept it in her backpack."

"I'll pass that along, but I'm pretty sure they would have found it if it was there."

"Well, I can give you the information on her emergency card," said Lucy, pulling out the file folder and opening it up. "Mr. and Mrs. John Whitney," she read, trying very hard not to think of the smiling couple in the photograph on Tucker's desk.

"Thanks, Lucy," said Barney, when she had finished.

"Who's going to call them?" asked Lucy. "Will it be you?"

"I hope not." Barney sighed. He had knocked on too many doors late at night, bringing bad news. "I sure hope not."

"Me too," said Lucy, feeling a surge of anger as she replaced the receiver. It was bad enough the murderer had taken Tucker's life, but whoever it was had done more than that. So many people would be affected: the little children in the day-care center who had come to trust and love Tucker; Sue would not only have to cope with her own grief, but she would have to find a new assistant; the police officers would have to struggle with their own emotions as they investigated the case. Everyone in town would be touched by this violent death in some way. Women who had walked alone at night without giving their safety a thought would now look uneasily over their shoulders. At home, they would be extra careful to make sure the windows and doors were locked at night. Children would be warned not to talk to strangers. No one would be able to rest easy, Lucy realized, until the strangler was caught.

She refiled Tucker's emergency folder and snapped the cabinet shut, making a little vow to herself. Tucker's murderer would be found and punished.

CHAPTER SIX

14 days 'til Xmas

The next morning, after Bill had left for work and the bus had carried the kids off to school, Lucy found herself alone in the house. Usually she enjoyed these few quiet early-morning moments, sitting down at the kitchen table with a second cup of coffee and planning her day. She reached for her calendar and opened it — Christmas was only two weeks away, she realized with a shock, and her shopping was far from done. She still only had one present for Elizabeth, the earrings, and didn't have the slightest idea what else to get her.

Lucy pushed the calendar away. It might be December, all right, but it sure didn't feel like Christmas. Not with Tucker dead. Things like that shouldn't happen. Young girls shouldn't die, but it was especially cruel when it happened this time of year.

Tucker had a mother and father who had

undoubtedly been making their own Christmas plans. Her father perhaps looking forward to a game of indoor tennis with his best girl, or maybe even a skiing trip. Her mother had probably been fussing over what to buy her for Christmas, just as Lucy was worrying about what to give Elizabeth. Or perhaps she had found just the right present and had tucked it away, carefully wrapped in jolly, holiday paper.

How did people stand it, wondered Lucy. How did they manage to go on living after losing a child? Worst of all for Tucker's parents, thought Lucy, was the fact that she had been murdered. It would be hard enough to accept the loss of a child in an accident, but how did you deal with the knowledge that somebody had killed your precious daughter on purpose?

Unable to sit still any longer, Lucy pushed the chair back and stood up. She reached for the sponge and began wiping the counter, pacing back and forth the length of the kitchen. She tossed the sponge in the sink, spotting a gaily decorated tin that had gone unnoticed in the ever-present clutter, tucked away on top of the cookbooks.

Curious, Lucy opened it up and found a carefully arranged assortment of cookies from the cookie exchange. Puzzled, she furrowed her brow. Finally the light dawned. Someone, probably Franny, had put them aside for Marge.

No time like the present, thought Lucy, as a plan took shape. She'd been intending to visit Marge, anyway, and now she had a good excuse. And since Marge was married to Barney, she might have some inside information on the police investigation.

"Barney didn't have much to say about it," said Marge, straightening the scarf she was wearing to hide the effects of the chemotherapy. She was lying on an aging plaid Herculon couch, with her shoulders propped on a pile of cushions. "I think it upset him, her being so young and all. And anyway, the state police handle all the homicides."

"I know," said Lucy, taking a seat in the rocking chair. Somehow it seemed presumptuous to sit in Barney's big recliner. "But they use the local manpower, too. For routine things like questioning neighbors, running background checks. Did Barney happen to mention who's in charge of the investigation?"

Marge's expression brightened. "He did mention Lieutenant Horowitz, I think. He's usually the one they send."

Lucy recognized the name. Her most recent encounter with the lieutenant had been the year before, when she was a member of the library board of directors and there had been some trouble.

"He's very thorough," said Lucy, remembering that Horowitz had even considered her a possible suspect. "I wonder if they have any suspects yet? You know, I heard she was involved with Steve Cummings."

As she spoke, Lucy suddenly realized that Steve was the most likely suspect. The husband, or in this case, boyfriend, always was.

"That nice dentist?" Marge raised her eyebrows.

"That nice dentist walked out on his wife and two adorable little girls," said Lucy. "Lee was pretty upset with Tucker at the cookie exchange."

"I don't blame her," said Marge. "Though by rights he's the one she should be angry with. And what's a man of his age doing with a young girl like Tucker anyway?"

"That seems to be the fashion nowadays. I guess it's some sort of status symbol to have a young girlfriend." It was that very generation gap, thought Lucy, that could cause problems in a relationship. Problems that could lead to murder.

"Nothing new about that," sniffed Marge. "It must be awful hard on their kids. Little girls, you said?"

"Hillary and Gloria. Gloria goes to school with Zoe, and Hillary's in the day-care center."

Marge clucked her tongue. "I suppose she has to work now that they're separated, but I don't see why these young mothers can't spend a few years at home with their little ones."

"They all have careers," Lucy said, remembering little Will's asthma attack the day before. "You know, I was helping Sue at the center yesterday, and Will Scott got sick. Sue had to take him to the emergency room, but when I called his mother she acted as if it was all a big inconvenience. She told me I should have called her husband."

"I guess I'm old-fashioned," said Marge, with a shrug. "I was raised that you never bothered a man at work. When Eddie broke his leg, I took him over to Doc Ryder. When the water heater broke and flooded the cellar, I was the one who called the plumber and got it fixed. Barney never knew what happened 'til it was all over and done with."

"Steffie's not like that, that's for sure," said Lucy. "But she takes an interest in

Tom's work — she's real active in Mothers Against Drunk Driving."

"Now that's something I don't hold with," said Marge, lifting a glass of water from the coffee table and taking a long drink. The table was filled with the clutter of illness: pill bottles, a heating pad, information pamphlets, and instruction sheets. "A man's work is his own business. Barney does his job, and I do mine. 'Course now it's different because I'm sick, but I always used to have a nice hot dinner on the table and a smile on my face when he came home from work. But I don't bother him about what he did or who's in trouble. If he wants to talk about it, fine, but I don't press him. It's hard enough being a cop, but he only has to do it forty hours a week. The rest of his time is his."

"It is a hard job, isn't it? After all, people don't call the police when everything's going great."

"That's for sure," agreed Marge. "But just between you and me it's worse than ever now that Tom Scott is the big cheese in the department."

Lucy couldn't help smiling. She hadn't heard that expression in years. "What's the problem?"

Marge shrugged. "Tom's got all these

ideas about how Barney should improve his outreach program."

"Really?" Barney was the department's safety officer, and through the years Lucy had seen most of his presentations at the school. "He does a great job, and the kids love him. That bike-safety obstacle course, where he sets up the real traffic light, they all look forward to that. He always does it the first day after spring vacation."

Marge's face softened. "Barney loves it, too. You know, he made all those signs and the traffic light — spent one whole winter down in the cellar, building all that stuff." She sighed. "Traffic safety, stranger danger, all that's old hat according to Tom. He wants more antidrug and antialcohol education."

"For kindergarten?"

"Can't start too young, I guess. Gotta scare 'em straight. At least that's what he tells Barney."

"Gee, whatever happened to childhood innocence? We used to try to protect kids."

"That's what Barney says, but Tom's given him these curriculums he's supposed to use. Big, thick books." She glanced at the recliner, where a special pocket held the TV remote. "Barney's not much of a reader."

Lucy chuckled, recognizing the truth of

Marge's statement.

"Actually," continued Marge, leaning forward, "I'm kind of worried. The more Tom leans on Barney, the more Barney resists. I'm afraid he's gonna snap and do something he'll regret. If he lost his job, I don't know what we'd do. We really need the medical insurance." She touched the scarf, reassuring herself that it hadn't slipped. "The surgery, the treatments, it's all very expensive."

"I wouldn't worry. Barney's got lots of seniority. I don't think they could fire him."

"I'm not worried about that, Lucy. I'm worried that he'll quit."

"He wouldn't do that — I can't imagine him as anything but a cop. It's what he is." Lucy patted her chest. "It's part of him."

"He keeps threatening. . . ."

"I think he's just talking." Lucy hoped it was true; she knew how vital medical insurance was. She and Bill had been unable to afford it themselves until the Chamber of Commerce set up a plan for members who were self-employed, like Bill. Before that, a case of pneumonia one winter had forced them to depend on food stamps and a loan from Bill's parents. Bill had only lost a few weeks of work, but the hospital had demanded payment and threatened legal action.

"Hey, did you hear about Richie?" asked Lucy, eager to switch to a more positive subject. "He got into Harvard."

"That's wonderful," enthused Marge, relieved to have a new topic of conversation. "Of course, he's always been a bright boy. What are Toby's plans?"

"He says he's interested in several colleges, but he's being awfully lazy about the applications."

"Who can blame him?" Marge rubbed her forehead and Lucy suspected she was getting tired. "I tried to help Eddie, but I couldn't manage it."

This was news to Lucy. She had thought Eddie would probably get a job after high school or join the armed forces. "Where's Eddie applying?"

"Culinary school. He wants to be a chef."

Lucy was impressed. "That's a good idea. He's worked at the Greengage Cafe for a couple of summers, hasn't he?"

"He loves it. But he says he has to go to culinary school to be a chef."

"Maybe I could help," offered Lucy. "The boys could work on their applications together. It might be just what Toby needs to get his done, too. Eddie could come over one day next week."

"That'd be great, Lucy. You could help him with the essay part since you write for the paper and all."

"I'll do what I can." Lucy checked her watch. "I've got to get going. I've got a list of errands a mile long."

"Thanks for coming, and thanks for the cookies." Marge nodded at the tin on the coffee table.

"Is there anything I can get you before I go?"

"No, Lucy, I'm fine."

"You take care now," said Lucy, giving Marge a quick hug before she left. Then, heading downtown, she thought about their conversation.

She sympathized with Marge, but she also knew that under the leadership of Chief Crowley, whose health had been declining for years, the Tinker's Cove Police Department had settled into a long slumber. Maybe Tom Scott would bring some much-needed vigor to the department.

Then, rounding a corner, she drew up short, noticing Steve Cummings's dental office. Acting on impulse, she pulled into the drive and parked in the small parking area behind the building. She hadn't gotten much information from Marge. Why not question her prime suspect directly?

As she made her way up the neat brick path to the door she tried to think of an excuse for seeing the dentist. Have her teeth cleaned? Dr. Cummings probably had a dental hygienist who handled that chore, and, besides, she would probably have to make an appointment. A cleaning was hardly an emergency.

Could she claim she had a toothache? A really bad one that needed emergency attention? The idea made her uneasy. If Steve Cummings had murdered Tucker, she hardly wanted to put herself at his mercy in a dental chair.

No, she would have to try a different approach. By the time she pulled open the door she had a plan.

"Do you have an appointment?" inquired the woman behind the desk. She was a rather heavy, middle-aged woman with brass-colored hair cropped in one of those upswept styles that was supposed to make a woman of a certain age look younger. It made this woman look like a Marine drill sergeant, thought Lucy.

"No, I don't. I'm from *The Pennysaver,* you know, the newspaper?"

The woman's face hardened. "We don't advertise," she said. "It's a matter of professional ethics."

"Oh, no. I'm not selling advertising. I write for the paper. I'm Lucy Stone."

The drill sergeant was not impressed with this information.

Lucy smiled, and plunged ahead, improvising as she went.

"Actually, I'm working on a feature story. We're asking prominent citizens, you know, people our readers will recognize, what they want for Christmas. It's kind of a man-in-the-street thing, with kind of a new twist? It'll only take a minute of the doctor's time."

"I don't think so." The drill sergeant shook her head. "In fact, Dr. Cummings has cut back his schedule today. He's only seeing a few patients whose treatment can't be delayed."

"Could you just ask him for me?" persisted Lucy. "In my experience, most of the people we interview for stories like this are pleased and flattered by the attention."

"I don't think that would be the case here." The receptionist's tone was flat.

"You never know. He might be upset if he learned you'd sent me away," suggested Lucy. "It's good publicity, and it's free. . . ."

Just then the door behind the receptionist's desk opened and Dr. Cummings appeared in his white jacket, followed by an elderly woman who looked a bit dazed.

"Ruth, I want you to make another appointment for Mrs. Slade here. Preferably next week." He handed a chart to the receptionist and quickly consulted a clipboard, then turned to Lucy. "Mrs. Green?"

"Oh, no," Lucy said quickly, before the receptionist could get her two cents in. "I'm Lucy Stone, from *The Pennysaver.*"

She watched his face closely, looking for a reaction, but Steve Cummings wasn't giving anything away. He looked the same as always, a thirtysomething professional with thinning hair and wire-rimmed glasses, except that today his eyes looked tired.

"I'm doing a feature story about Christmas, and I'd just like to ask you a few quick questions, if you don't mind?"

"Sure. Come on in."

Lucy followed him, making a point not to look at the receptionist. She knew looks couldn't kill, but she wasn't taking any chances.

He led her into a small office, with a large desk. He seated himself behind it, and Lucy took a chair.

"It's just a man-in-the-street sort of thing," she began, letting her hands flutter in front of her. "I'm supposed to ask various important people, you know, people our readers will recognize, what they want for Christmas. You can be as serious or as funny as you want to be. And, of course, I have to take your picture."

She bent down to fumble in her purse for her notebook, all the time keeping an eye on Dr. Cummings. He leaned back in his chair, folding his arms behind his head.

"What I want for Christmas, eh?" He sighed, and a shadow seemed to pass over his face. Then he focused his eyes on her. "There's something I always wanted, ever since I was a kid, but I never got. My parents didn't think it was appropriate: a G.I. Joe doll. They didn't approve of dolls for boys, but I'm telling you, they made a big mistake. I saw one at an antique show not long ago, and it was worth a bundle."

Lucy smiled and scribbled down his quote. Actually, she thought, this could turn out to be a good idea for a story. But before she left, she had another question she wanted to ask. She pulled her camera out of her bag and waved it apologetically in front of her face.

"Now's the tough part. I have to take your picture."

"Go ahead. Shoot."

She glanced around the room. "You're against the window — that doesn't work.

Could you stand against the wall?"

"Oh, sure." He got up and moved into position, straightening his jacket and smiling.

"You know, I really lucked out with this assignment. I was afraid I'd have to cover that murder," volunteered Lucy, from behind her camera.

"That was a terrible thing," said Steve. His smile was gone. He looked as if he was going to cry.

"Oh, I'm sorry," said Lucy, lowering her camera. "I didn't know you knew her."

"Only slightly." Steve's expression became guarded. "But I have a wife and two daughters. I don't like the idea of something like this happening in Tinker's Cove."

"I'm surprised to hear you say that." Lucy smiled mischievously at him. "I was at a party with Lee a few nights ago, and it didn't sound as if she would mind if you were murdered one bit."

He gave a hollow chuckle. "I guess that's par for the course. We're separated, you know, but hopefully we'll work things out."

"Hopefully." Lucy raised the camera again. "Now think of those two beautiful daughters of yours." His face brightened, and he smiled; Lucy snapped the photo.

"Thanks so much for your time," she said,

starting to pack up her camera and note-book, when the door flew open.

The receptionist was clucking nervously, like a hen spying a hungry dog on the other side of the fence. No wonder, thought Lucy, recognizing the man behind her: Lieutenant Horowitz, the state police detective.

"I was just leaving," said Lucy, heading for the door.

"Good idea," said Horowitz, making eye contact with her. "This is the last I want to see of you Mrs. Stone. Do you understand?"

Lucy hastened to reassure him. "Yes. Yes, I do. I'm gone. You won't see me again."

"I hope not." Horowitz pulled his long upper lip down, and pressed it against his bottom lip. It made him look a little bit like a rabbit. Then he turned. "Dr. Cummings, I have a few questions for you. . . ."

So, great minds think alike, thought Lucy, pushing the door open. She wasn't the only one who suspected Cummings. Pausing for a moment on the stoop, she surveyed the scene. Not only did she recognize the detective's gray sedan, but two cruisers were also parked on the street in front of the office. Horowitz had brought reinforcements.

She slung her shoulder bag up over her arm and started down the path to her car. What she wouldn't give to hear Horowitz's questions.

But as she started her car, she couldn't help harboring a few doubts. Somehow, Steve Cummings just didn't seem like a murderer to her.

CHAPTER SEVEN

As she headed downtown to the dry cleaners, Lucy tried to sort through her confusing thoughts. Logically, she knew Steve was the obvious suspect — boyfriends and husbands accounted for the great majority of murdered women. Her instincts, however, told a different story. Steve had seemed friendly and open, he hadn't seemed like a man with a death on his conscience. And even if all the terrible things Lee said about him were true, which Lucy doubted, there was no question that he adored his little girls. She couldn't forget the way his face had brightened when she told him to think of Hillary and Gloria when she snapped his picture.

Lucy pulled into a free parking space and picked Bill's good sport coat off the passenger seat. She sat there, holding it in her lap, wondering if she could really trust her feelings about Steve. Murderers, she knew, didn't come with handy identifying marks on their foreheads. Mostly, they were ordinary people who had snapped for one reason or other: sweet-faced young baby-sitters who had shaken a crying baby a bit too hard, frustrated boyfriends whose anger had gotten out of control, battered wives who hadn't seen any other way out.

Just because Steve seemed like a perfectly nice guy didn't mean he couldn't have murdered Tucker. Lucy didn't have access to the evidence, she didn't know what Lieutenant Horowitz had found at the crime scene. All she had to go on was her gut feeling, and that didn't count for much in a court of law. She sighed and opened the car door.

Inside the little shop, with its strong chemical scent, Lucy had to give her name and phone number.

"I thought I knew most people in town," said the clerk, with a little sniff.

"We're not regular customers," explained Lucy, taking the little pink slip. "Most of our clothes go in the washing machine."

As she pushed open the door and headed back to the car, she decided to pay a visit to the person who knew Steve best: Lee. It wasn't as if she was getting involved in the case, she told herself. Not at all. She had a very good reason for stopping in the decorating shop where Lee worked. Since Bill was going to have to repair the dining-room ceiling, anyway, they might as well freshen the room up with some new wallpaper.

Captain Crosby Interiors occupied one of the big old houses on Main Street, in fact, it had been occupied briefly by Captain Elisha Crosby after his marriage to the lovely Betsy Billings. Local legend had it that he kissed Betsy good-bye one fine February morning in 1886, promising to return by Christmas with a hold full of China tea, and was never heard from again.

Nowadays, the fine old house was an ideal setting for the shop, which sold fabrics and wallpapers. Lee had worked there part-time for years, mostly as a hobby, but had switched to fulltime after the separation.

When Lucy entered, Lee was busy with a customer so she gave her a little wave and settled herself down with the wallpaper books. As she flipped the pages, she tried to think of a graceful way to bring up her questions about Steve. After all, just because Lee wasn't very happy with him these days didn't necessarily mean she would welcome the idea that he was a suspect in a police investigation.

As it happened, however, Lucy didn't have to find a way to work the murder into the conversation after all. Lee couldn't wait to talk about it.

"Lucy!" she exclaimed, after her customer had left. "Did you hear about Tucker?"

"Isn't it terrible," murmured Lucy.

"You won't find me shedding any tears for that little hussy," declared Lee. "If you ask me, she got what she deserved. I don't know if you knew, but she'd been trying to steal Steve away from me."

"I'd heard something like that," admitted Lucy. "Was it serious? I mean, do you think Steve was planning to marry her?"

Lee snorted. "That little snippet? I don't think so. Not that she wasn't trying. And it wasn't just Steve, either. She was doing her darnedest to turn Hillary against me."

Lucy's chin dropped. "What do you mean?"

"At the day-care center. She always made a huge fuss over Hillary. Big hellos and good-byes, even hugs and kisses. It was a bit much, if you ask me. Oh, I know you're not supposed to speak ill of the dead, but this is one death that couldn't have happened to a nicer person."

Lucy was glad she was already sitting. If she hadn't been, she would definitely have needed a chair. Lee's attitude would have knocked her off her feet.

"Aren't you worried that the police might suspect Steve?" she asked.

"Steve?" Lee thought this was hilarious. "Are you kidding? He couldn't even drop a lobster into a pot of boiling water. I always have to do it."

Lucy looked at her curiously, and Lee gave her head a shake.

"Listen to me, going on like this. You didn't come in here to talk about my marriage. What can I help you with? Wallpaper?"

"For the dining room. Since we have to fix the ceiling anyway, I thought we might as well do the whole room."

"Good idea! I have just the thing. It would be beautiful in your house."

Lee pulled a book out from beneath the counter and set it in front of Lucy. With a flourish, she revealed a bright Oriental design featuring enormous, brightly colored peacocks.

"Isn't that gorgeous? That blue! And the green and the pink. Go for it, Lucy. People are so afraid of color. It's a big mistake when it can bring life and excitement to your home."

"I was thinking of something more . . . beige," said Lucy.

"Beige?" Lee was disappointed.

"Maybe a stripe," suggested Lucy.

"I've got it." Lee pulled out another book. "Wainscoting! That way you can have your cake and eat it, too. Color on the bottom of the wall, something light and airy above."

"That's a good idea," admitted Lucy, intrigued.

"It would be nothing at all for Bill to put up a little bit of molding."

"It would really dress up the room. I'll think about it. Can I take the book?"

"Sure." Lee drew closer and lowered her voice. "Don't tell anybody I told you this, but I can probably do something for you on the price. We have a big sale after Christmas, anyway."

"Thanks, Lee. I'll get back to you as soon as I can."

"There's no rush. Take your time."

Lucy couldn't swear to it, but she thought Lee was humming a happy little tune as she saw her to the door.

"Have a nice day, now, you hear."

As she walked down the pathway to her car, Lucy was so deep in thought that she didn't notice Lieutenant Horowitz approaching.

"I seem to keep running into you," he said, eyeing her with disapproval. "And I don't think it's a coincidence. I'm beginning to suspect that you're conducting your own investigation of Tucker Whitney's death."

Lucy looked up, startled. "I'm sorry. What did you say?"

"I said I think you ought to mind your own business instead of poking your nose into an official police investigation, that's what I said."

"Oh, I'm not. . . ."

"Don't give me that," growled Horowitz. "I know what you're up to, and I'm warning you that you could be breaking the law."

Lucy smiled sweetly, and held up the wallpaper book as proof of her innocence. "Buying wallpaper is against the law?"

"No, Mrs. Stone. There's no law against buying wallpaper, but there are plenty of laws about obstructing justice."

"Well, I happen to be interested in wallpaper," said Lucy, allowing a self-righteous tone to creep into her voice.

"Right," muttered the lieutenant, brushing past her and pulling open the door to the shop.

Lucy continued on her way to her car, checking her watch as she went. It was later than she thought, she realized, thinking guiltily of the long list of Christmas errands she hadn't done. With only two weeks left until the holiday she'd wasted an entire day running around town looking for information, and she didn't even have the comfort of knowing she'd made any progress. The sun was already setting, a giant red ball sinking behind the stark, black silhouettes of the bare trees, and she had more questions about Tucker's murder than she'd had that morning when she set out. All she'd managed to accomplish, she realized, was to antagonize Lieutenant Horowitz. Now, the kids were home from school and she had to get home, too, and put that roast in the oven if they were going to have it for supper.

CHAPTER EIGHT

13 days 'til Xmas

Today was another day, another chance to tackle that list of errands, resolved Lucy as she started the car on Friday morning. If she didn't get anything else done, she definitely had to get the Christmas cards mailed. Then she had to go to the bank, get gas and groceries, and stop at the church to pick up Zoe's angel costume for the Christmas pageant.

As she drove down Red Top Hill and turned toward town and the post office, she remembered that she only had a few dollars in her wallet. She turned and was driving down Main Street, approaching the rec building on her way to the Seamen's and Merchants' Bank, when a huge Ford Expedition suddenly pulled out in front of her, directly in her path.

Lucy slammed on the brake and held on to the steering wheel for dear life, narrowly missing a collision. As she watched, horrified, the Expedition almost tipped over as the driver made a sharp turn into the narrow street. For a second or two it was only on two wheels, then the driver gained control and it righted itself. As it sped down the street past her, Lucy got a clear view of the operator. It was Lee.

Making a quick decision, Lucy flipped on her blinker and turned into the rec-center parking lot Lee had just exited. She must have just dropped Hillary off at the day-care center; maybe Sue would know what was going on.

"I haven't got a clue," said Sue, who was on her knees struggling to unzip Hillary's jacket. "Mommy was in a hurry this morning, wasn't she?"

After a few more tugs the zipper opened, and Hillary shrugged out of her jacket and ran across the room to join Emily at the toy stove.

Sue examined the zipper, fingering the place where the fabric was torn.

"I don't know what's going on, but this obviously wasn't a good morning for Lee. She just shoved Hillary through the door and left, never said a word."

"She was driving like a maniac when she left here. Almost ran right into me."

Sue shook her head. "Maybe she's finally realized that Steve's a suspect in the murder. Last night Horowitz paid me a visit and all his questions were about Tucker's relationship with Steve."

"He's the obvious suspect. Obvious to everyone except Lee."

"Oh, I don't know. It seemed to me that he and Tucker were more good friends than anything else. Tucker told me she liked him and all, but she thought he was too old for her. She said it was like dating her father!"

"Maybe Tucker wasn't serious, but Steve was," suggested Lucy. "Sounds like a motive to me."

"Could be." Sue glanced around the room, making sure the children were all behaving themselves.

Lucy took the cue. "I've got to go — have a nice weekend."

"It doesn't look too good right now. Tucker's parents are coming to make funeral arrangements — the service is going to be on Monday night — and they want to meet with me."

Sue's expression was grim, and Lucy knew she was dreading the meeting.

"Will you be all right? Do you want me to go with you for moral support?"

"Thanks, Lucy," said Sue, squeezing her

hand. "This is something I have to do alone. I'll be all right."

"Okay. Call me if you change your mind."

Back in the car, Lucy tried to sort out her thoughts. From what Sue said, it seemed that Steve was definitely the prime suspect. Horowitz had questioned him, he'd questioned Lee, he'd even questioned Sue about Steve's relationship with Tucker.

Lucy tried not to think about how likable she'd found Steve, she tried not to think about how happy Lee had been to have Steve all to herself again, she tried not to think about little Hillary and Gloria. Whatever was going to happen was out of her hands. If Horowitz had the evidence, there was no doubt he would arrest Steve Cummings.

All weekend, Lucy followed the newscasts. She tuned in while she drove Sara and Zoe to their friends' houses on Saturday, she listened to the radio while she cooked supper that night. On Sunday morning she was so eager to see the paper that she went out to the plastic tube that stood by the road in her slippers, even though there were two inches of snow. Her feet got cold and wet, but she didn't learn anything new. Police were reported to be continuing the investigation, but there were no new breaks in the story.

On Sunday afternoon, she and Bill left the kids home and went to the mall in Portland to finish their Christmas shopping. Bill was happily humming along to a favorite Clapton tune when Lucy switched the radio to the all-news channel.

"Why'd you do that?" he asked.

"I keep waiting to hear if they've arrested Tucker's murderer," she explained.

"I'm sure they'll break in with an announcement if that happens," he said, switching back to the local music station. "Why don't you just sit back and enjoy this rare opponunity to be alone with me? I'm your favorite husband, after all."

"Okay," said Lucy, laughing, and temporarily shelving her intention to talk to him about Toby. "It's just you and me and a very long shopping list."

At the mall, Lucy couldn't help thinking that Bill looked a little out of place in the trendy juniors shop, a refugee from the granola wars in his beard and corduroy slacks, topped with a plaid flannel shirt and a bulky down jacket. He surprised her when he pointed to a sparkling spandex T-shirt and suggested they buy it for Elizabeth.

"That?" Lucy raised her eyebrows doubt-fully. To her, it looked-sleazy. Besides, it was overpriced at thirty-nine dollars.

"She'll love it," he said, nodding positively. "I saw something just like it on MTV. And it's on sale."

He was right, Lucy realized, spotting a sign indicating the whole rack was one-third off.

"That makes it . . ." She furrowed her brow as she figured the math.

"About twenty-four dollars."

"Okay." Lucy pulled the shirt from the rack.

Now, on Monday afternoon, as she tucked tissue paper around the shirt and arranged it in the box, she couldn't help smiling fondly. That was the thing about Bill. He kept surprising her. Married for almost twenty years, and he hadn't lost the power to amaze her. That itself was astonishing, she thought, picking up the ringing phone.

"Oh, Lucy," wailed Sue. "It was awful."

"What was?"

"Tucker's parents came."

Lucy sat down on the bed, remembering how worried Sue had been on Friday after-noon. It seemed like eons ago.

"That must have been sad. Were they real

emotional?"

"That was the worst part. They're terribly polite, you know, and very stiff-upper-lip and all that. But you could tell they were all ripped up and torn inside. They should have been beating their breasts and sobbing, but instead they were telling me they didn't want to intrude and would only take a minute but they did want to gather up Tucker's belongings and by any chance, if it wasn't too much trouble, could I tell them a little bit about her work at the center?"

"What did you say?"

"What I told you. That she really seemed to enjoy her work and that I don't know what I'll do without her." Sue paused. "They wanted to know if she'd seemed troubled or anxious — they really seemed to want to know about that."

"Of course they would."

"I couldn't bring myself to tell them anything about Steve — I just said I hadn't noticed anything wrong. I should have noticed something, shouldn't I?"

"Don't blame yourself," said Lucy. "What could you have done? You didn't even know about Steve until she told you on the way to the cookie exchange."

"If only she'd confided in me sooner. I could have advised her, warned her to be careful. I don't know."

"Well, Steve is the last person you'd think to warn her about," said Lucy, matter-of-factly.

"You think it really was him?"

"I'm not convinced, myself, but I think it's just a matter of time until he gets arrested. What I can't figure out is what's taking the police so long."

Sue was silent for a minute. Finally, she spoke. "Well, at least then the Whitneys will know what happened to Tucker. They say that the trial brings a sense of closure to the victim's family."

"I wish I believed that," said Lucy, remembering Tucker's bright presence at the cookie exchange. "I don't think parents ever get over the death of a child. Oh, they go on living, but they're never the same. It's like they're walking wounded."

"You're right." Sue's voice was so sad that Lucy struggled for some way to console her.

"You gave her something wonderful, you know. You gave her the job at the center and she discovered her vocation — that she wanted to work with kids. She loved working at the center, everybody says so. And she was perfect for it. She was bright and happy and full of energy." Lucy paused, hearing the kids arriving home from school in the kitchen downstairs. "That's how I'm going to remember her. Now, I've got to go. It sounds as if the Mongol hordes have found the refrigerator."

"I better let you go, then." Sue sniffled. "Thanks for everything, Lucy. Talking to you really helped."

"Anytime. Now, for my next challenge: preventing World War III."

In the kitchen, Lucy found Eddie and Toby with their heads buried in the refrigerator. Elizabeth was perched on the counter, legs crossed, doing her best to catch Eddie's eye. Sara was prying open a yogurt carton, not having bothered to remove her coat, and Zoe was precariously balanced on a kitchen chair trying to reach the cookies in the cabinet high above the stove.

"Hi, Eddie," began Lucy. "Elizabeth — off the counter. Zoe, don't climb on chairs, it's dangerous. Sara, hang up your coat. Toby, reach that bag of gingersnaps for me."

Lucy set out a plate of cookies and poured big glasses of milk for the boys. Elizabeth didn't want any; she fled from calories like a vampire avoided the rays of the sun. Sara took the yogurt into the family room and Zoe renewed her efforts to scale the kitchen cabinets, this time looking for the chocolate syrup.

Lucy pried her loose and joined the boys at the kitchen table, planting Zoe in her lap.

"So, are you going to work on those college applications today?" she asked. She turned her gaze on Toby. "As I remember, you owe me one, and today's a good day to make good."

Toby grimaced and popped a cookie in his mouth. Eddie shifted his bulky frame in the chair and leaned back, brushing his crew cut with his hand. Lucy was struck yet again by how much he resembled his father, Barney.

"You don't want to be a cop, like your dad?" Lucy realized she had spoken without intending to.

Eddie's face reddened; he looked uncomfortable. "Nah," he finally said, reaching for another cookie.

"He just likes to eat — that's why he wants to go to cooking school." Toby punched Eddie's shoulder.

Lucy shook her head. They might be bigger, she thought, but they behaved just like the little Cub Scouts who used to cluster around her kitchen table every week.

"Did you bring the applications?"

Eddie nodded and pulled a thick sheaf of

papers from his backpack.

"Well, it looks as if you guys have your work cut out for you. Why don't you get started — just jot down some ideas for those essays. I'll see how you're doing in about half an hour, OK?"

"Sure thing, Mom," said Toby, pulling his own pile of papers toward him and opening the top folder.

"Call me if you get stuck," she said, heading downstairs to the washer and dryer.

From time to time Lucy peeked in the kitchen and saw the boys bent over the table, apparently deeply immersed in the applications. When she noticed it was beginning to get dark, she decided to ask Eddie to stay for dinner. But when she went into the kitchen she found the boys had disappeared, leaving the papers behind. Leafing through the printed forms she saw that only the most basic questions had been answered; there was no sign of any progress on the questions that required essays.

"January 1. These are due January 1," she muttered to herself, looking out the window.

There was no sign of the boys in the yard, so she checked the family room and went upstairs to peek in Toby's room.

"Have you seen Toby?" she asked Elizabeth, who was reclining on the couch in the family room and flipping through channels with the remote. "By the way, don't you have any homework?"

"Nope. Tomorrow is 'Smart Kids, Smart Choices.' "

"What's that?"

Elizabeth pulled a wad of folded paper from her pocket. "Don't read the back, OK?"

"Scout's honor," said Lucy, carefully prying the layers apart and studying the Xeroxed notice.

"Smart Kids, Smart Choices," she learned, was made possible by the Tinker's Cove Police Department and the PTA. This traveling troupe of reformed alcoholics and drug abusers, none older than twenty-five, would present a "hard-hitting, graphic account" based on their own experiences. The rest of the morning would be spent in discussion groups and in the afternoon the entire school population would work together to create message murals that would be displayed in the halls.

"This is taking all day?" asked Lucy. "What about French and chemistry and algebra and . . ."

"Oh, Mom," groaned Elizabeth in a world-weary voice. "If they actually taught us chemistry, we'd probably just cook up our own drugs. That's what they think, anyway."

"Well, maybe if they taught you some solid reasoning skills, they wouldn't have to indoctrinate you and you could figure out for yourselves that drinking and using drugs isn't very smart."

"Interesting, Mom," said Elizabeth. "Very interesting." She studied her fingernails, which were painted light blue. "But hopelessly retro."

"That's me. Hopelessly retro," agreed Lucy, who had received a solid prep-school education and could still conjugate her Latin verbs, even if her inability to comprehend percentages had been the despair of the entire math department. She resolved to call the principal for a little chat, in which the school's declining SAT scores would definitely be mentioned.

Failing to find the boys in the house, Lucy concluded that they must be outside. She stood in the kitchen doorway and yelled for them. Their heads popped out from behind the shed, only to disappear immediately.

What are they up to? she wondered, pulling on her jacket. She marched across the yard, straight to the shed.

"What are you guys doing? Are you smoking?" she asked, suspiciously.

126

This last was met with gales of laughter. Laughter that didn't stop, but rolled on, eventually forcing the boys to clutch their stomachs and sides. There was also a sweet, familiar scent in the air.

"Pot!" exclaimed Lucy. "You've been smoking pot!" Suddenly Toby's odd behavior made sense, including the disappearance of her Dee-Liteful Wine Cake.

"Shhh, Mom. Not so loud." Still shaking with laughter, Toby put a finger over his mouth to caution her.

"I can't believe it!" She shoved Toby in the direction of the house. "How stupid are you? Don't you know you could get in big trouble?"

Eddie and Toby glanced at each other and dissolved into giggles.

"Where did you get it?"

"It's all over the school, Mom," said Toby. "You can get whatever you want."

"You can? Like what?"

"Uppers, downers, heroin, crack . . ."

"Crack!"

"Yeah, Mom. Crack."

"You've actually seen crack?"

"Well, no," admitted Toby. "But I've heard about it."

"And who's the person who's got all this stuff?"

Now the boys weren't giggling. Their glance was an agreement not to reveal any names.

"Okay, okay," said Lucy, backing off. She shook her head. "Boy, your dad is not going to like this."

"Mom — you're not gonna tell Dad, are you?"

"Of course I am. And Eddie's dad, too."

"You can't do that, Mom," begged Toby. "Dad's already pissed off at me."

"And my mom's sick and all — this'll kill her," added Eddie.

Lucy took a deep breath. "Okay," she finally said. "I won't tell anybody, but you have to promise not to do this again. Ever. OK?"

The boys nodded.

"Now, inside. I'm going to make some coffee."

It was all she could think of that might counteract the effect of the marijuana and return the boys to their normal state. Not that they seemed to be out of control. They were content to sit at the table, watching her scoop instant coffee into mugs with bemused expressions on their faces.

"I can't believe you're this stupid," she hissed at them. "Especially after what happened to Tim Rogers. He got himself into a mess of trouble, and you could, too, if you get caught with marijuana."

She poured hot water into the mugs, set them in front of the boys, then made one for herself.

"And you've wasted the whole afternoon," she couldn't help adding, glancing at the unfinished applications. "Don't you want to get this over with and get those darned things in the mail?"

Toby shrugged and shoveled several spoonfuls of sugar into his mug. "I don't know, Mom. I don't know if it's worth it."

"What do you mean?" Lucy was puzzled. "You have wonderful opportunities ahead of you." She glanced at Eddie. "Both of you. You're lucky you have families that will help you get the educations you want."

"Dad's not so keen," said Toby, stirring his coffee.

"My dad isn't either," admitted Eddie.

"That's not exactly true," said Lucy, with a flash of insight. "They just don't want to admit that you're growing up."

Toby sook a slurp of coffee. "Really good, Mom. Reeelly good. Taste it, Ed."

Eddie gulped down half a cup and smiled. "Yeah, man. Good."

Lucy sighed. "Well, I guess you're not going to finish these today." Lucy gathered up the papers.

"What's the point?" asked Toby. "Look what happened to Tim."

"Yeah," agreed Eddie. "He trained all year long. Made All-State and MVP. And then they took away his scholarship. Over nothing."

"He lost his scholarship? Because he was arrested?"

"Bastards took it back," fumed Eddie.

Lucy was seized with the desire to grab the two boys by the scruffs of their necks and knock their heads together. Instead, she counted to ten. Then she spoke.

"You don't get it, do you? Tim broke the law, that's why he lost the scholarship. He got drunk and he drove the car and he got caught. It's nobody's fault but his own. Get that straight."

But looking at them, she knew they didn't believe her. To them, Tim was just proof that the harder you tried, the more you had to lose. Therefore, you might as well not try in the first place.

Finishing her coffee, she revised her earlier opinion of "Smart Kids, Smart Choices." Maybe it wasn't such a bad idea after all. It certainly couldn't hurt, she thought, watching as the boys finished off the last of the gingersnaps.

CHAPTER NINE

"You'll ruin your appetites." Lucy couldn't help saying it, even though she didn't think it mattered much to the boys whether they had room for dinner or not.

Dinner, she realized with a start. She'd forgotten all about it. She had to get the chili cooking, and then she had to do something about getting Eddie home. Normally, Toby would drive him home in her car, but she couldn't let him do that while he was still feeling the effects of the pot. She would have to do it herself.

"I'm really angry with you," she told Toby. "Now I have to rush to get dinner made because I have to drive Eddie home. I can't believe you boys are so inconsiderate, so irresponsible."

"Don't mean to be, Mom," said Toby, brushing away a tear. He was clearly coming down from his high, ready to wallow in depression.

"Get out of here," said Lucy, losing patience. "I'll call you when I'm ready to go."

The boys thumped up the back stairs to Toby's room, and soon Lucy heard the repetitive thumps of a rap CD. Scowling to herself, she pulled a pan out of the cupboard and began browning a couple of pounds of ground turkey. While it cooked, she chopped up some onions, then added them to the meat along with some chili powder. She dumped in a few cans of beans and tomatoes, gave the whole mess a stir and covered the pot, setting the heat on low. Then she went in the family room to assign one of the girls to watch the pot.

Before she could ask Sara to keep an eye on the chili, Toby and Eddie thundered into the room.

"You can't stop us, we're so tough we'll drop ya . . ." they chanted together in rap style, hunching up their shoulders and leaning forward, stepping from side to side in unison.

"Mom, Eddie and Toby are acting weird," said Sara.

"They're just fooling around," said Lucy.

"Toby was crying — I heard him." The expression on Sara's round little face was serious. "And they ate all the cookies."

Lucy didn't know what to say. She certainly didn't want to give Sara the true explanation for the boys' mood swings and extraordinary appetites.

"They're worried about getting into college," she finally said, glancing at the dancing duo. "Stress can make you do strange things. Listen, Peanut. I have to get some milk, so I'm going to take Eddie home. Will you watch the chili for me? Give it a stir now and then and if it looks like it's cooking too hard, just turn the stove off. OK?"

"OK, Mom."

"C'mon boys — it's time to go." Lucy herded the two gangsta rappers out of the family room and into the kitchen, where she handed them their jackets.

"Have you got all your stuff?" she asked Eddie.

"Yeah. I think so," said Eddie, taking his backpack from her.

She was sure he didn't have a clue. In fact, neither did Toby. The two were standing in the kitchen, waiting to be told what to do next.

"Car."

They nodded and shuffled out the door. She followed, shaking her head. It must be true, she thought. Pot today must be stronger than it was when she was in college. She'd smoked it a few times herself back then, but she didn't remember it having much of an effect.

Getting the seat belts fastened seemed to be quite beyond both boys so Lucy helped strap them in. Just like when they were little, she thought. Only then they were cute; now they were really beginning to get on her nerves. She climbed in behind the wheel and started the car. Her favorite classical radio station came on and the boys groaned, so she switched to WRPP, their favorite, to pacify them.

A song, or something like a song, was just ending, and the five o'clock news was next. After a string of commercials for cars, soft drinks, and a record store, they heard the familiar voice of deejay Fat Fred.

"We start tonight's news with a live report from Tinker's Cove, where state police have arrested dentist Steve Cummings, charging him with the murder of Tucker Whitney last Wednesday. State police Lieutenant Horowitz made the announcement just moments ago."

Lucy's right hand left the steering wheel and rested on her lips, she used her left hand to pilot the car down the driveway and on to Red Top Road. As much as she expected this turn of events, it still shocked her. She listened to the sound bite with

Horowitz's voice.

"The swift conclusion of this investigation was possible largely due to the efforts of the Tinker's Cove Police Department; in particular the crime-scene management of Lieutenant Tom Scott made possible the preservation of crucial evidence."

Then it was back to Fat Fred, who said Dr. Cummings would be arraigned in superior court the next morning.

Wow, thought Lucy. She'd never known Horowitz to share credit for an arrest. Wasn't Barney always complaining that while the local cops did much of the grunt work in criminal investigations the state police always acted as if they'd done everything?

"Say, man, isn't that your dentist?" Toby asked Eddie.

"Whuh?"

"Who's your dentist?" persisted Toby.

"Dr. Cummings." Eddie gave him a big smile, revealing massive blocks of gleaming tooth enamel. "He's OK, for a dentist."

"Yeah, right. He just got arrested for murder."

"No way." Eddie shook his head.

"Way, man," said Lucy. "Way."

When Lucy got home, she found Bill sniffing a gallon container of milk.

"Sara said you went out to get milk, but we have this and part of another. Is there something wrong with it?"

"Uh, I guess I didn't see it," said Lucy, realizing she had been caught fibbing.

Just then, Toby shuffled into the kitchen, muttering under his breath. Bill glanced at him curiously.

"Actually, I forgot all about the milk. I came straight home because Toby said he was feeling kind of sick."

Lucy attempted to make eye contact with Toby, and jerked her head toward the stairs.

"I think you'd better go lie down. Right, Toby?"

"Whuh?"

"Lie down. I think you have a little fever. You'll feel better when you wake up."

Much to her relief, Toby disappeared up the back stairway. Bill watched him go, then turned to Lucy.

"Is something going on that I ought to know about?"

"I don't think so," said Lucy, checking on the chili. She lifted out a fragrant spoonful. "Here, taste this. Tell me what you think."

She held the spoon and Bill took a bite. "Mmmm."

"Mmmm good or mmmm needs something?"

"Mmmm good."

Hearing a clattering sound, Lucy and Bill turned toward the stairs. Toby staggered back into the kitchen and plopped himself in one of the chairs.

"When's dinner, Mom? I'm starved."

His eyes were abnormally bright. Lucy noticed and so did Bill. He bent down and studied them.

"Are you on something?" he asked suspiciously.

"Nah, Dad."

"I think he has a little fever," said Lucy, making a show of placing her hand on Toby's forehead.

Bill planted his feet in the middle of the kitchen and stared at Lucy. Then he turned his gaze on Toby. He shrugged and reached for his jacket.

"I'm not a fool," he said, and walked out the door.

Dinner, without Bill and with Toby's odd behavior, was an experience Lucy was only too happy to forget. It was almost enough, she decided as she slipped behind the wheel of the Subaru, to make Tucker's memorial service seem an attractive prospect.

But not quite enough, she decided, when she took her seat in a pew at St. Christopher's Episcopal Church. Bending her head, she recited the Lord's Prayer in an effort to focus her thoughts. She was here to remember Tucker, not to fret about her own problems at home.

She raised her head and listened to the organ music. There, in the front row, she saw a well-groomed couple accompanied by two teenage boys with shining caps of blond hair. Tucker's parents and her brothers. She hadn't realized Tucker had two younger brothers. Tears sprang to her eyes, and she screwed them shut, covering them with her hand.

When the tears stopped coming Lucy reached in her pocket for a tissue and wiped her eyes.

"Tough, isn't it?"

Lucy looked up and saw Sue taking the seat next to her. She nodded, and Sue took her hand. Sue's face, Lucy saw, was wet with tears, and she passed her a clean tissue.

I hope I brought enough, thought Lucy, realizing that the service was going to be a tearful affair. But if she was honest with herself, she thought, she couldn't be sure if she was crying for Tucker or for herself.

How could Toby be so thoughtless? So irresponsible? Didn't he know that whatever he did affected the whole family? What about the girls? They deserved a brother they could be proud of. And what about her and Bill? Didn't Toby know how much they loved him, how much they wanted him to be successful and happy? She looked at the Whitneys, bereft of daughter and sister. But people didn't have to die to be lost. Drugs could take away a beloved child just as surely as any murderer. Lucy tightened her fists, making her knuckles white. She wouldn't let that happen to Toby she promised herself. She would do whatever she had to do.

Her eyes fell on Tom and Steffie Scott, sitting together a few rows down. Maybe she should tell Tom about Toby. He'd know what to do.

She considered the idea. It would be such a relief to get the whole thing out of her hands. To pass it on to somebody who dealt with these problems every day. But was Tom the right person? What if he arrested Toby and he ended up in jail?

Lucy found herself shaking her head. She needed to slow down, she decided. Of course she was upset. But this was the only time she'd known Toby to use drugs. For all she knew, it was the first time. And it was only pot. It wasn't as if Toby was a drug addict; she'd been overreacting.

Tomorrow the whole school would be participating in "Smart Kids, Smart Choices." Maybe it would help Toby understand what a dangerous game he was playing. Lucy watched as Barney and Marge made their way down the aisle, taking seats near Tom and Steffie and the other police officers.

It wouldn't hurt to wait a bit, she decided, as the organ music stopped. And in the meantime, she could let Barney know she was concerned about the drugs in the high school without going into any specifics. After all, she would see him tomorrow at the kindergarten Christmas party. With that settled, she turned her attention to the service.

"Tonight," began the priest, "we are gathered together to celebrate the life of Tucker Whitney . . ."

Much to Lucy's relief, Bill was asleep when she got home. After the heartbreaking memorial service she really didn't want to get into an argument with him. She knew she ought to tell him about the marijuana, but she also didn't want to go back on her word to the boys. It was an impossible position, and she knew it. She never should have promised to keep it a secret.

The next morning was much too busy for any kind of serious talk — she had to pack lunches and make breakfast and, as it happened, Bill had an early meeting with a drywall contractor. The only bright spot, she thought as she hurried through her morning routine so she wouldn't be late for the kindergarten Christmas party, was that Toby didn't seem to be suffering any lasting effects from yesterday's experiment with illegal substances. Still, as she parked the Subaru outside the elementary school, she was determined to talk to Barney about the easy availability of drugs in the high school.

She was rushing up the stairs to the school, fumbling in her shoulder bag for her camera and reporter's notebook when she ran straight into Lee Cummings.

"You're the last person I expected to see today," said Lucy, blurting the words out before she thought and then feeling horribly embarrassed. "That came out all wrong, Lee. What I meant to say is that I know this must be an awful time for you."

"I'm here for Gloria," she said in a subdued voice. "I know a lot of the kids have probably heard about Steve's arrest. I'm trying to keep things as normal as possible."

"It must be hard on the girls," began Lucy, as they walked down the hallway to the kindergarten classroom.

"You have no idea," said Lee, biting her lips. "What really hurts is that we'd decided to get back together."

Lucy raised her eyebrows in surprise.

"It's true. Steve and I talked when I got home from the cookie exchange, and he admitted he'd been a jerk and said he just wanted for us all to be together as a family again." She sighed. "I guess it'll be a while before that happens."

They had reached the kindergarten room, but before Lucy could push open the door Lee stopped her.

"Lucy, you've solved a few crimes in the past. You could figure out who really killed Tucker. Would you do it? Would you help Steve?"

Lucy's mouth dropped open. "Gee, I don't know. . . ."

"You could do it. Say you will. Please."

"Oh, Lee, I'm not on the police force. I don't know what evidence they've got, but Horowitz sounded pretty positive at that press conference that he had the right man."

"But they don't, don't you see? Steve was coming back to me. He was done with

Tucker."

Lucy groaned inwardly. "Don't *you* see? That could be his motive. Maybe Tucker didn't want to let him go. Maybe they fought and he got angry and ended up killing her."

"Well, Lucy, if you think that, you sure don't know Steve. He'd never hurt anybody; he's really committed to healing. Back when a lot of dentists were refusing to treat patients with AIDS, it was just never an issue for him. He never turned anyone away, not anybody, even if they couldn't pay."

Lee pulled the door open and marched into the classroom. Lucy followed, wondering if she had a point. She wondered if the police really had a case against Steve or if they'd simply arrested the most obvious suspect.

"Welcome to our classroom," said Lydia Volpe, indicating Lucy and Lee with a nod. "There are chairs in the back of the classroom."

Lucy searched the room for Zoe and found her sitting beside her best friend, Sadie Orenstein. Gloria, Lee's little girl, was just behind them. Lucy gave them a smile and a little wave as she took her seat. As she expected, there was no sign of Barney yet. He would make a surprise appearance as

Santa Claus after the children finished presenting the songs and fingerplays they had been practicing for weeks. Of course, all of the children knew what to expect, thanks to older brothers and sisters. The Christmas party was a Tinker's Cove tradition, and local merchants generously donated toys and books for Santa to distribute. Lydia made sure that Santa knew in advance which children weren't likely to have very lavish Christmases at home so especially nice gifts could be given to them.

As always, the program was adorable, and Lucy had no trouble filling a couple of rolls of film with cute pictures. Ted often said you couldn't have too many photos of dogs and children in a community newspaper so she was sure he'd be pleased with her work.

Finally, when the children got to the last line of "Up on the rooftop, ho, ho, ho," the door flew open and Barney made his entrance, dressed in a Santa Claus suit that was beginning to look a bit worse for the wear, his familiar face hidden behind an elaborately curled, enormous fake beard.

"Ho, ho, ho!" he roared, and the children erupted into giggles and screams and jumped up and down with excitement. A few bolder children, children Lucy suspected didn't get much attention at home,

144

wrapped their arms around his massive, treelike legs and hugged him.

"Children." After twenty years in the classroom, Lydia's voice commanded attention, and the children quieted down. "If you will take your places, I believe Santa may have some presents *for good boys and girls. Is that right, Santa?*"

"Yes, it is, ho, ho, ho. I have a pack filled with presents for *good little boys and girls.*" Barney turned his back, showing the bulging sack he was carrying.

There was a mad scramble as the children ran for their desks, anxious to get their presents as soon as possible. When it was quiet, Barney seated himself and plunked his sack down between his legs. Then he pulled out a long list, unrolling it with a dramatic flourish.

"Jason Adams."

Jason, a little boy with a huge gap in his front teeth, jumped to his feet and ran up to Santa. Barney fumbled in his bag and presented him with a festively wrapped, flat package. Jason hurried back to his seat and began opening it. Every eye was on him. When he finally got it unwrapped he shrugged philosophically.

"It's a coloring book," he said. "With crayons."

Nobody seemed very impressed. They turned to Barney, waiting to see what the next present would be.

"Susanna Barlow," said Barney, pulling out another package that looked very much like the first. He gave it to Susanna, a little girl with freckles and long braids.

Lucy happened to know Susanna's grandmother, Dot Kirwan, who worked at the IGA. Dot was the first to admit she shamelessly spoiled her first grandchild, and Susanna was an expert at opening presents. She ripped the paper off in no time, revealing another coloring book and crayons. Scowling, she clumped back to her desk and mashed the wrapping paper into a ball.

The children began to fidget in their seats, growing restless. It was one thing to sit quietly, anticipating a terrific present like a Barbie doll or a soccer ball, but it was very hard to sit still for what they were all beginning to suspect was only a coloring book and a box of six no-name crayons.

"Justin Diggs."

As soon as Lucy heard the name she knew Barney was in trouble. Justin lived out on Bumps River Road in a hardscrabble neighborhood where the tired houses were surrounded with cars that didn't go and appliances that didn't work. This was probably going to be his only Christmas present, and he had been expecting something good.

"Justin, go and get your present from Santa," prompted Lydia.

Justin stayed put at his desk. "I don't want no coloring book. My brother got a Mighty Morphin Power Ranger last year. I want somethin' like that."

Lydia glanced at Barney, whose Santa beard didn't begin to hide his unhappiness, and took swift action.

"Santa, would you mind distributing the presents to the children? That would be quicker, I think, and the mothers can begin setting up the refreshments."

Taking his cue, Barney went from desk to desk passing out the coloring books. He kept up a brave front, issuing lots of ho-ho-hos, but Lucy knew his heart wasn't in it. He loved playing Santa and hearing the oohs and aahs and squeals of delight when he passed out the presents, and this year there were only a few polite thank-yous.

When the refreshments had been served and the children were busy licking the icing off their cupcakes, she approached him.

"What happened? No donations this year?"

"I had to refuse 'em. Orders from the top."

"What?"

147

"Lieutenant Scott. He said it wasn't appropriate for the safety officer to act like the Salvation Army. Told me to give out anti-drug coloring books instead."

Lucy picked up one of the coloring books that had been abandoned on a nearby desk and flipped through it. When she got to the outline of a hypodermic needle with a big X through it she groaned and put it back down.

"My word," she said, shaking her head. Her first impulse was to sympathize with Barney, but then she remembered Toby and Eddie's little experiment with pot the day before. "Maybe Tom Scott is on the right track after all. . . ."

She was interrupted by Lee.

"Barney Culpepper, I have to talk to you."

"Fire away," said Barney, with a sigh.

"Maybe Santa could continue this conversation outside," suggested Lydia. "I think it's time to wrap things up."

A quick glance around the room was enough for Lucy. The little natives, fueled by sugary treats, were getting restless.

"I hope you have recess next," she told Lydia.

"Are you kidding? Today is double recess." Then she raised her voice, making an announcement to the class. "Children, I'm afraid Santa has to go back to the North Pole now. What do you say?"

"Thank you, Santa," chorused the little girls and a few boys.

"Thanks for nothing, Santa," grumbled Justin. This was met with hoots of approval by the children.

"Merry Christmas, everyone!" roared Barney, turning and striding out of the room. A quick exit was definitely his best option.

Lucy hurried down the hall after him, determined to share her concern about the drug situation at the high school, but she didn't catch up to him until he was outside, by his cruiser, pulling off the Santa outfit.

"Hey, you're going to blow your cover," she joked.

"I think it's blown," he said, rolling the red suit into a ball and tossing it into the trunk.

"You know, what I started to say inside is that this antidrug campaign may not be such a bad idea. I think it's really needed." She took a deep breath and forged ahead. "From what I hear, the high school is full of illegal substances."

Barney snorted. "Stop the presses," he said.

"What do you mean?"

"Lucy, this isn't exactly news, you know.

The whole town's full of the stuff." He shook his head. "I've never seen it so bad."

That wasn't quite what Lucy expected to hear. Nevertheless, she plunged on. "Well, if it's true, then isn't it important to educate the kids about drugs so they'll know not to use them?"

Barney threw up his hands in dismay and stood facing her, arms akimbo. "Let me tell you something, Lucy. All that education stuff sounds good in theory, but you know what, it doesn't work. The only thing that does work is keeping the drugs out, cutting off the supply. And as long as the only way a lobsterman can make a living is by bringing 'em in, well, we're not gonna be able to keep the drugs out. Too much money in 'em, and a man who's having trouble feeding his family or making the payment on his boat isn't gonna say no."

"I guess you're right."

"You know it." Barney pulled his heavy belt, complete with gun holster, out of the trunk and strapped it on. "Maybe there is something you could do, though."

"What?" Lucy asked eagerly.

"It isn't just drugs, you know. The kids especially get into trouble with booze. You know about Tim Rogers?"

Lucy nodded.

"Well, we're having a sting operation. Richie Goodman is going to try to buy booze, and if they sell it to him, we're gonna issue warnings. It could make a good story for the newspaper."

"Sure. Just let me know when, okay?"

"Deal." Barney slammed the trunk shut and pulled open the car door, but he wasn't quick enough to avoid Lee, who had followed them out of the school.

"Barney, I've got to talk to you," she demanded, grabbing his arm. "You know Steve's innocent, don't you?"

"We-e-ll," began Barney, looking more than ever like a worried St. Bernard. He shook his head dolefully. "I gotta tell you, it doesn't look good for Doc Cummings."

"They've arrested the wrong person, I'm telling you," insisted Lee.

Barney nodded sympathetically. "I know how you feel, but they've got some pretty convincing evidence."

Lucy leaned closer. "What is this evidence?" she asked.

Barney scratched his chin underneath the fake beard. "Fibers, skin cells, a gum wrapper."

"A gum wrapper? They're accusing my husband of murder because of a gum wrapper?" Lee was incredulous.

"Sugarless," said Barney. "With finger-prints."

Certain he'd clinched the case against Cummings, he climbed into his cruiser and drove off, leaving Lee and Lucy on the sidewalk.

"Because it's sugarless gum, it has to be a dentist?" Lee's voice dripped with sarcasm.

"He did mention fingerprints," said Lucy.

Lee dismissed that evidence with a wave. "Listen. I know Steve Cummings better than anyone, and I say, sure, he's a two-timing bastard and a lying, cheating son of a bitch and I wouldn't trust him with another woman as far as I could throw him, but he's no murderer!"

CHAPTER TEN

As she started the Subaru, Lucy couldn't help smiling. This was more like the Lee she knew. Outspoken, outrageous — you had to love her.

Lucy's next stop was the photo shop, where they promised to develop her film right away. Then she was off to *The Pennysaver* to write up a story about the Christmas party.

This was going to be a bit sticky — Ted was expecting a happy holiday feature about cute little kiddies receiving gifts from Santa. But that wasn't what really happened at the party. She didn't want to embarrass Barney, but she had an obligation to tell the truth.

The jangle of the bell and the sharp scent of hot lead that still lingered years after the linotype machines had been removed always had the same effect on her: It was something akin to the reaction a racehorse has to the sound of the trumpet. She sailed past Phyllis, the receptionist, giving her a wave, and plopped herself down in the chair Ted kept relatively clear for his visitors.

"I think I've got something . . ."

"Santa Claus is a fake?" asked Ted.

"Well, kind of. Something like that might work for a headline," said Lucy, ignoring his sarcasm. "There were an awful lot of disappointed little kindergarteners at the school this morning. They all got antidrug coloring books instead of the usual gift bonanza. Barney said it was a policy decision by the lieutenant. I think it might be a significant story, considering the town's drug problem."

Ted considered her pitch.

"I dunno. Somebody must have donated those coloring books. We don't want to insult them. After all, Santa Claus did come, and the kids did receive gifts. Some readers might think the kids are just ungrateful."

"You know that's not true," argued Lucy. "Those coloring books are the only gifts some of those kids are going to get this Christmas, and they were expecting real presents, just like in the past."

"I know." Ted chewed on a pencil.

"And Barney says all this drug education is a lot of nonsense anyway. He says the town is full of drugs because of the lobster quota."

Ted pushed his chair away from the antique rolltop desk he had inherited from his grandfather, also a small-town journalist, and laughed.

"Lucy, this is not the *Washington Post* or the *New York Times*. We're a small-town weekly that depends on local advertisers. It's bad enough we have a young girl murdered by the local dentist, but now you want me to print that the town is full of drugs, too? Believe me, I hold my breath every time we get a press release from the state police drug task force — and so far, I've been lucky. Nobody from Tinker's Cove has been arrested. And believe me, this is one issue I'm not going to touch until I have to. If a handful of lobstermen are bringing in drugs to pay off their mortgages and keep shoes on their kids' feet, well, who am I to start pointing fingers? Folks around here have always done what they had to to get by."

"I get your point," said Lucy, holding her hands up in surrender. "It's smiling faces and ho-ho-hos all around."

At her desk, she flipped through the press releases Phyllis had collected for her, looking for possible future stories. Nothing

155

looked very interesting: the annual holiday bazaar at the Community Church, a Christmas dinner for people who would otherwise be alone sponsored by Alcoholics Anonymous, and a batch of used-clothing and used-book sales. Barney's sting operation, a community taking care of its children, was beginning to look better all the time. She picked up the phone and dialed the police station, intending to ask Barney for the date and time.

"Lucy?" Barney sounded defensive. "I can't talk about the Christmas party."

"I know. Don't worry. Ted wants a heartwarming holiday story, and that's what he's going to get."

"That's a relief." Barney expelled a great sigh — it sounded like a tornado on the telephone.

"This is off the record," she began, sensing that now that he was no longer worried about looking like the Grinch in the newspaper he might be more talkative than usual. "You know how convinced Lee is that Steve is innocent? She asked me to look into it and . . ."

"Oh, no." Barney cut her off. "Don't do that, Lucy."

"I wasn't intending to." Lucy was quick to tell him, her voice rising in pitch. "But I just wanted to know — for my own peace of mind — are you guys sure you've got the right man?"

" 'Fraid so." Barney lowered his voice. "I tell you, Lucy, morale around here is pretty high. Never been higher. You heard about Horowitz? Congratulatin' the department? That's never happened before. And you know why? Because the guys from the fire department, the EMTs would be all over the place before we could secure the scene. Chief Crowley knew it was no good, but he'd just say, 'What can you do? Ya gotta try to save the victim, even if the victim's beyond saving.' But now the lieutenant's in charge, it's different. This one was by the book and whaddya know? It worked. We're not the Keystone Kops anymore."

Lucy looked up as Phyllis deposited the packet of pictures on her desk.

"I don't think people thought you were Keystone Kops."

"Believe me. We took a lot of grief from the state police, even the cops in other towns."

"I didn't know that." Lucy ran her finger under the flap to open the packet. "So, what about the evidence that was so carefully preserved? What was it?"

"Oh, I dunno. Crime-scene experts took

care of that. There were fibers, I guess. All that microscopic stuff. And the gum wrapper, o' course, with Cummings's fingerprints."

Lucy pulled out the pictures and saw Steve Cummings's smiling face looking up at her. She'd forgotten all about taking his picture on Friday. Now, she remembered telling him to think of his girls. The trick had worked; she'd caught him looking particularly attractive.

"What about time?" she asked. "That kind of physical evidence could have been left anytime, and everybody knows he was seeing her."

"Nah," protested Barney. "They have ways of dating it. Plus, Cummings doesn't have an alibi for the time of death on Thursday morning. Shoulda been at his office, but he wasn't."

"Oh." The longer Lucy looked at Steve's picture, the less she thought he had murdered Tucker.

"That's how you build a case, you know," said Barney, sounding rather pompous. "Bit by bit. In the end, it all adds up."

Lucy suspected he was reciting something he'd heard, perhaps a lecture by the lieutenant on the proper handling of evidence.

"Well, thanks a lot, Barney. I feel better.

But it's still hard to believe Steve Cummings could do something like that."

"See, that's where amateurs go wrong," said Barney. "You think a person's innocent because you know them, and they're nice. From what I hear, Ted Bundy is a heck of a nice guy, a real charmer, but he killed a bunch o' women, didn't he? Nope, you can't trust people, but you can trust the evidence."

Lucy chuckled. "Okay. I give up. Now, when is that sting operation?"

"Lemme see." Lucy could hear rustling paper. "It's Thursday night. Is that good for you? Seven o'clock."

"Great." Thursday night gave her almost an entire week to write the story before the next Wednesday deadline. Plus, it would be a heck of a lot more interesting than that dismal dinner. "See you then."

She hung up and studied the photo of Steve Cummings. She had taken it under false pretenses and the last thing she wanted was for Ted to run it with the story about Steve's arrest, so she quickly tore it into small pieces and tossed it into the trash. She turned her attention to the pictures of the children, writing brief captions for the best ones. Then she quickly typed out a few paragraphs about the party, focusing on the children's songs and the refreshments provided by the mothers. She played Santa's arrival up big and played down the presents. When Ted read it he was pleased as punch.

"Just one question . . ." he began, exercising his editorial prerogative, as Lucy answered the ringing phone.

She held up one finger, indicating she would be with him in a minute.

"*Pennysaver,* this is Lucy."

"Thank God you're there!"

"Sue?"

"Can you come over? I'm desperate!"

"Right now?"

"Yes. It's Will. Another attack. I've got to take him to the clinic."

"Okay. I'm on my way."

Lucy expected to find the day-care center in chaos when she got there, imagining small figures running around and shrieking at the top of their lungs. All was quiet, however, when she pulled open the door. Connie Fitzpatrick, one of the teachers at Kiddie Kollege, the nursery school that was also housed in the rec building, had settled the children down for their nap.

"Hi, Lucy," she whispered. "Sue says they rest for at least a half hour, but if they fall asleep they can go 'til one-thirty."

Lucy nodded and Connie tiptoed out, leaving her in charge. She hung up her coat and checked on the children, who were lying on floor mats. Her buddies Harry and Justin were sound asleep, and Emily seemed ready to drift off. Hillary, Lee's little girl, was lying on her back, holding up a stuffed toy and whispering to it.

Lucy caught her eye and held her finger to her lips, warning her to be quiet. Hillary rolled over on her tummy, hugging the little bear and sticking her thumb in her mouth.

Continuing her circuit of the room, Lucy felt a bit non-plussed. She had expected to have to cope with a difficult situation but everything was under control. She looked out the window for a few minutes, then went over to Sue's desk, looking for something to read.

She picked up a magazine and sat down in the rocking chair. But somehow she couldn't get interested in whether she should "Take the Plunge! Go for the Gold!" and color her hair blond. As for "Paint Your Way Out of the Box!," well, her house was hardly a surburban box and, while the dining room definitely needed work, she didn't think she was interested in knocking even more holes in the plaster for an antique look and applying a faux marble finish.

She dropped the magazine in her lap and leaned back, closing her eyes and intending to relax, but it was no good. Her eyes refused to stay shut, and her legs twitched. She needed to move. She got up, stretched, and walked back to the window. She stayed there for a few minutes, doing squats to relieve the tension in her legs. Then she replaced the magazine on Sue's desk and stood for a moment at Tucker's.

It was now bare; her parents had taken her things. Lucy pulled out the chair and sat down. With nothing better to do, she opened the shallow center drawer, releasing the bitter smell of unfinished wood. As she expected, the drawer was empty, as were all the others. But when she tried to close the big bottom drawer it wouldn't go all the way in.

Getting down on her hands and knees, Lucy pulled the drawer out and peered behind it. Something was stuck in the space behind the drawer. She reached in and felt a plastic-covered book of some kind. The missing agenda, she thought, with a rising sense of excitement.

She pulled it out, discovering the bright pink, chunky day planner Sue had described. No wonder they hadn't been able to find it; as long as it remained upright, there had been enough room for the drawer to close. It was only when it fell on its side that it blocked the drawer.

Lucy set the agenda on the desk and replaced the drawer. Then she sat down once again and held the agenda, smoothing it with the palm of her hand. Should she open it? Some people used agendas like diaries, recording intimate details of their lives. Tucker, Lucy guessed, wasn't like that. She probably used her agenda as a calendar, so she wouldn't forget meetings and appointments.

It wouldn't hurt, thought Lucy, to take a peek. If it seemed personal and private, she could stop. But when she leafed through the lined pages she found only the briefest notations. On the day she died, Lucy discovered, Tucker had been planning to get a haircut at five-thirty.

Curiously, Lucy leafed through the pages preceding her death. They were mostly blank. The cookie exchange was noted, as was an oil-change appointment. And Tucker had planned something for Sunday, but Lucy wasn't sure what. In her clear, precise block printing she had written three letters: A, M, and C.

What did that mean, wondered Lucy. Was

she planning to meet somebody? Somebody with the initials AMC? Who could that be? And when? Tucker had not written down any time, which seemed odd.

Unless, thought Lucy, it was such an important meeting she didn't have to. Her parents coming, perhaps? Or a serious boyfriend. Those weren't Steve's initials, that was for sure.

Not Steve, thought Lucy, struck with a horrible realization. Not Steve's, Lee's. Aurelie Mabelline Cummings. Lucy mouthed the words, silently. Then she picked up a pencil and wrote the initials on a scrap of paper: A. M. C.

Lucy's eyes fell on little Hillary, now sound asleep on her mat. She had the awful feeling she was looking at a motive. Just how far would Lee go to get Hillary and Gloria's daddy back? Lee had made no bones about the fact that she hated Tucker; could she have killed her?

Seeing Sue's face in the glass window of the door, Lucy rolled the paper into a ball and tossed it into the wastebasket. Her first impulse was to get rid of the initials; she wasn't ready to think about this now.

"Hiya," she whispered. "How's Will?"

"Better." Sue sighed and sat down in the rocking chair without taking off her coat.

"I'm exhausted."

"Racing off to the clinic with a sick child will do that to you," observed Lucy.

"It's really not fair," complained Sue. "If his folks weren't in denial about this whole thing, and if they started treating Will's asthma, I wouldn't have to go through this every other day."

"The doctor will talk to them."

Sue shrugged. "That's the problem with the clinic. It's a different doctor every time."

Lucy looked at her watch. "I have to go."

Sue nodded. "Thanks for helping out."

"No problem. Oh, by the way. I found Tucker's agenda. It was stuck behind a drawer."

"Always the detective." Sue smiled at her.

"I was bored." Lucy blushed.

"I'll send it to her folks."

Lucy nodded, relieved. That took care of that problem. "Thanks," she said, and hurried out to her car.

Today, she definitely wanted to be home when the kids got home from school. Considering yesterday's happenings, she didn't trust Toby and wanted to keep an eye on him. She also knew she had to tell Bill about the marijuana, and figured things would go better if she broached the subject after he'd had his favorite dinner: meat loaf.

She was in plenty of time, as it turned out. The Regulator clock in the kitchen read two o'clock when she got home, giving her at least an hour before the kids would arrive. Plenty of time to fix herself a belated lunch. But when she opened a cabinet to get a clean glass, she noticed the light on the answering machine was blinking. She punched the button and listened, while she poured herself a glass of milk.

"Mrs. Stone, this is the Tinker's Cove High School. Please report to the assistant principal's office before the end of the day."

"Toby," groaned Lucy, replacing the milk container and slamming the refrigerator door shut. She took the glass of milk with her, to drink on the drive. She was pretty sure she would need nourishment to face what was coming.

CHAPTER ELEVEN

Calls involving the assistant principal never meant good news. The principal saved all the good news for himself; he issued all the congratulations and honors leaving the assistant principal, Mr. Humphreys, to handle disciplinary matters.

It was ironic, thought Lucy. Toby had always had a blameless disciplinary record. But just as he was applying to colleges and would need faculty recommendations, of course now was the time he chose to get himself into trouble.

What had he done? It hit Lucy like a semi speeding down Red Top Road at ninety miles an hour: He had got caught with pot.

Her stomach twisted itself into a knot, and she regretted the milk she'd gulped while speeding along. A drug offense meant he was in big trouble. She struggled to remember the official school policy, clearly stated and sent home at the beginning of the school year with every student in the Tinker's Cove High School student handbook. If only she'd read the damn thing.

A detention or suspension wouldn't be so bad, but she had a horrible feeling that the school also took it upon itself to report drug offenses to the police. That could mean Toby would be charged with a crime. Could they send him to jail? With all those murderers and thieves and rapists. Not in my lifetime, vowed Lucy, determined to defend her child no matter what. Toby may have done something wrong, but he still had rights, and she was going to make sure he exercised them.

Stupid, stupid idiot, she muttered under her breath as she parked the car in front of the school, marched up the sidewalk and down the hall to Mr. Humphreys's office. She yanked the door open angrily and stopped dead in her tracks. It wasn't Toby sitting on the bench in Mr. Humphreys's anteroom, it was Elizabeth.

"What happened?" asked Lucy, sitting beside her. She felt completely off-balance. This wasn't what she had expected at all.

"I was only trying to help." Elizabeth was so angry her entire body was tense.

"Tell me the whole story."

"This girl named Chantal was having an

asthma attack, and I gave her my inhaler."

"Did it work?"

"Yeah. She's fine." Elizabeth was picking at the brown paper cover on a thick history textbook. It was filled with multicolored doodles and scribbles and was beginning to tear at the corners.

"So what's the problem?" Lucy didn't get it.

"Ah, Mrs. Stone. You're here." Mr. Humphreys was a tall man with a little potbelly. He had a wispy blond mustache and had trouble keeping his thick eyeglasses up where they belonged. They kept sliding down his oily nose. "Why don't we all come in my office and discuss this?"

Elizabeth rolled her eyes and got to her feet, sighing as she stood up. It was the official teen sigh, a protest against the stupidity of adult rules and regulations.

Lucy flashed her a warning glance and stepped into the office. Elizabeth followed, and Mr. Humphreys shut the door behind them. He oozed across the room and seated himself behind his desk, giving them a little smile. Lucy felt itchy all over.

"Ah, Mrs. Stone. I'm afraid what we have here is a very regrettable situation. Elizabeth was found in possession of a prescription drug, and she distributed it to a fellow student."

"It's my asthma inhaler, and I gave it to Chantal because she couldn't breathe and was turning blue." Elizabeth spat the words out.

"But the problem is that students are not allowed to carry prescription drugs without a note from the doctor. I checked with Mrs. Irving, the school nurse, and it seems you are not authorized to carry an inhaler. There is no doctor's note in your file."

"Surely that's a technicality," said Lucy. "I can tell you that Elizabeth has asthma and her allergist has prescribed medication, including inhalers. She is supposed to carry one all the time in case she needs a quick fix." Ooh, she thought to herself, that didn't sound good.

"That's very well and good, Mrs. Stone, but Elizabeth neglected to request a drug authorization form from Mrs. Irving and did not have the form completed and returned by the doctor. She is in clear violation of school policies. But what disturbs me even more is that she *distributed* a potentially dangerous drug to another student." Mr. Humphreys pursed his lips and fixed his eyes on Lucy, peering over his thick horn rims.

"Now, Mr. Humphreys, you know as well

as I do that there's a big difference between sharing an inhaler and selling crack cocaine. I'm sure Elizabeth was only trying to help — the girl was having trouble breathing."

"That's right!" interjected Elizabeth. "Mom, Chantal was really in trouble. Her fingernails were turning blue."

"Elizabeth has had attacks herself and has been taught to manage them," said Lucy. "It sounds to me as if she did exactly the right thing."

"Is Elizabeth a doctor?" Mr. Humphreys inquired sarcastically. "Is she qualified to prescribe drugs? I think not."

"Of course not," said Lucy, trying very hard to remain polite. "But only a handful of drugs are used to treat most asthma cases, and the inhalers are clearly marked by color. Kids who have asthma all know that the yellow inhaler is for emergencies. Considering Elizabeth's excellent academic record and the fact that she's never been in trouble before, I think you ought to make an exception in her case."

Mr. Humphreys made a tent of his fingers and slowly shook his head from side to side. "Mrs. Stone, our school board has adopted a zero tolerance policy toward drug use. That means there are absolutely no exceptions. That's what zero tolerance means. I don't think there is anything to be gained by continuing this discussion. Elizabeth clearly violated school policy as stipulated in the handbook. She will be suspended for two weeks and a report will be forwarded to the police department." He gave a little nod. "You can expect the police will want to conduct a thorough investigation."

"That's not fair!' Elizabeth was on her feet.

Mr. Humphreys glared at her from his seat. "Two weeks suspension plus one day, for disorderly behavior."

"Come on, Elizabeth." Lucy wrapped an arm around her shoulder and led her out of the office. "Let's get out of here."

As soon as they were in the hallway Elizabeth completely lost control. She jumped up and down in fury and shook her head, the sleek sophisticated hairdo began to fray as clumps of hair worked loose.

"Come on, baby. You can do that at home. In fact, I'll join you. But now we've got to get out of here before they call the cops on you."

"Mom, this is so unfair! I saved that girl's life. I did. She was in real trouble, and the teacher, it was a substitute, wouldn't let her go to the nurse's office and kept telling her to stop making a scene. If I hadn't given her my inhaler, she would have passed out for sure."

"I know you did the right thing." Lucy hugged her. "I'm proud of you. I'll always be proud of you. And we'll figure this thing out. In the meantime, look on the bright side," she said, pushing open the school doors. "You don't have to come back for two weeks."

Elizabeth shrugged and thumped down the steps in her clunky platform shoes.

Behind them, inside the school, Lucy heard the bell ring. She quickly followed Elizabeth to the car, hurrying to stay ahead of the flood of students that would soon come pouring out of all the exits.

The car was blocked in by a line of school buses, so Lucy and Elizabeth couldn't leave. They sat, watching as a steady stream of students flowed down the steps and onto the buses, keeping an eye out for Toby. When they spotted him, Lucy honked and Elizabeth stuck an arm out the window and waved.

"Hi, Mom. What are you doing here?"

"Elizabeth got suspended."

Toby's eyes almost popped out of his head, but he quickly recovered and climbed in the backseat, forgoing the usual argument about who was going to ride in the front seat.

"Good going, Lizzie. You were probably tired of being on the honor roll, anyway."

"Shut up," growled Elizabeth.

"Be nice, children," said Lucy, easing into the flow of traffic as the school buses began moving. As they inched along, Lucy replayed the meeting with Mr. Humphreys in her mind, deciding the whole thing was ridiculous. Ridiculous, she thought, and dangerous. She didn't like it one bit.

Neither did Bill when he heard the whole story at dinnertime.

"Elizabeth, it serves you right. This whole thing could have been avoided if you'd simply followed the rules and gotten a note from the doctor," he said, taking a big forkful of meat loaf and mashed potatoes. "But, frankly," he added, glowering at Toby, "you're not the one I thought would get in trouble for drugs."

Just then the phone rang, and he got up to answer it. When he returned to the table, he looked a bit shamefaced.

"That was Mrs. Williams, Chantal's mother. She said she wanted to let us know how much she appreciated Elizabeth's quick thinking. She's convinced Elizabeth saved

Chantal a trip to the hospital."

Later, while the kids did the dishes, Lucy and Bill remained at the table, drinking their coffee.

"What do we do? Do we fight this?" asked Lucy.

"I don't get it," said Bill. "From what Mrs. Williams said Elizabeth ought to be a hero. Instead, she's suspended. It's crazy."

"Mr. Humphreys said he's referring it to the police." Lucy furrowed her brow. "Maybe I should call Barney."

"Wouldn't hurt," agreed Bill. "And in the meantime, I'm going to have a talk with Toby, *mano a mano*. He's got to understand that if he keeps messing around with pot, he could get in real serious trouble."

He cocked an eyebrow and grinned at Lucy, and for a moment he reminded her of the college kid she'd fallen for so many years ago. A college kid who never passed along a joint at a party without taking a toke.

CHAPTER TWELVE

7 days 'til Xmas

When Lucy arrived at the police station on Thursday night to cover the sting operation she felt a bit uncomfortable. After all, until now no member of the family had been in trouble with the authorities. Tom Scott immediately put her at ease.

"I received that report from the school concerning Elizabeth, and I don't see anything for my department to investigate — she didn't break any drug laws." He gave her a big smile. "You ought to be proud of her — her quick thinking probably saved that girl an ambulance ride."

"That's a big relief," said Lucy, smiling as Barney and Richie Goodman entered Scott's office. Lucy had known Richie ever since he was a baby, but she was always surprised by how quickly kids grew up. She could have sworn he'd grown a foot since she last saw him. He was at least six feet tall, a lean, good-looking boy with a thick mop of curly brown hair.

"Now, Richie here is going to try to buy alcohol from license holders in the town," explained the lieutenant. "He's obviously underage — he's seventeen and the legal age is twenty-one. Richie, will you tell Mrs. Stone here what your instructions are?"

Richie looked embarrassed, but he spoke right up. "I'm supposed to ask for a bottle of beer, and if they sell it to me I'm supposed to bring it out to Lieutenant Scott. If they ask me for ID, I'm going to say that I don't have any."

"That's right. We want to do this thing fair and square," said the lieutenant. "Right, Culpepper?"

Barney shrugged and nodded. "Right."

Lucy didn't think he sounded very enthusiastic.

"Now, just to make it absolutely clear that we're not planting any alcohol on innocent license holders, I'm noting on the record of this operation that Richie does not have any alcohol concealed on his body. Do you want to pat him down, Mrs. Stone?"

Richie was blushing furiously.

"I think I'll leave that to Barney," said Lucy.

Barney quickly checked Richie's pockets

and confirmed that except for a wallet and car keys they were empty.

"We're off, then," said the lieutenant, grabbing his blue jacket from the coat stand in the corner.

They all piled into a cruiser: Barney was driving, and the lieutenant sat next to him in the front seat. Lucy and Richie were in the backseat. Lucy got out her reporter's notebook and uncapped her pen.

"Is this the first sting the department has conducted?" she asked.

"As far as I know," answered the lieutenant. "Officer Culpepper's the one to ask — he's been here a lot longer than me."

"It's the first," agreed Barney, sounding glum.

"Liquor stings have proved to be effective community policing — a lot of departments are trying them," said Scott, turning to face Lucy. "It lets licensees know that we're really serious about enforcing the drinking age. And that's a message we want to get out now, with the holidays just around the corner."

"If Richie is able to purchase beer, what will you do? Will you charge the license holder?" Remembering Ted's reluctance to offend the business community, Lucy hoped not.

"This time we're issuing warnings," said Scott. "And, of course, we're hoping that having this written up in the paper will also act as a deterrent. No community business-man wants bad publicity."

Lucy squirmed in the uncomfortable seat. She didn't like the feeling that she was be-ing used to punish local businesses.

Tom Scott seemed to sense her discomfort and hastened to reassure her.

"This is kind of a personal crusade for me," he said. "When I first started out in police work I felt the same way a lot of cops do — that my time and energy were best used to fight serious crimes. I tended to ignore minor violations in order to concen-trate on cases that involved bodily harm or violence — muggings, bar fights, things like that. Remember, this was in New York City, where there are a lot more crimes against people and property than there are here."

He paused a moment, and when he re-sumed his voice was strained.

"That all changed for me one night when I got a call to a motor-vehicle accident — a car had hit a light pole. This was in a sec-tion of the precinct where we were rarely called. A very nice residential area in the Bronx called Riverdale with fancy homes, lots of trees and grassy lawns, not exactly mean streets, if you know what I mean.

"Well, when I got to the scene I found a brand-new Mustang. . . ." Scott paused to swallow, as Lucy scribbled his story down in the notebook word for word. "I knew it was bad. Entire front end was gone, like it had disintegrated under the force of the impact. When I got to the car the windows were open, and I could smell the alcohol."

He sighed and shook his head.

"It was too late. There was nothing I could do. Two kids, both dead. All dressed up in their prom clothes. He was wearing a tux, she had on a long dress. Her flowers — white roses — were still on her wrist."

He paused, working his teeth.

"That night I had to stand on two door-steps, ringing the bell, knowing that the people on the other side of the door were never going to be the same after I delivered my news. It was then I decided that I'd had enough. I promised myself I was going to do whatever I had to do to stop this, this epidemic of alcohol abuse that is killing our young people."

In the front seat, Barney pulled a huge, white handkerchief out of his pocket and blew his nose. In the backseat, Lucy finished writing just as they pulled up in front of Mrs. Murphy's liquor store. She glanced over at Richie and saw his Adam's apple bob as he swallowed.

"Are you ready?" asked Scott.

"Ready as I'll ever be," answered Richie, climbing out of the car.

The others remained in the cruiser, watching as Richie approached the brightly lit store. He pulled open the glass door and went in. They could observe him through the plate-glass windows as he walked over to a cooler and chose a bottle of beer which he carried to the counter.

The clerk, an older man with gray hair, shook his head.

"That's Jim Murphy — he knows the business," said Barney, a note of satisfaction in his voice.

Tom noticed and looked at him curiously. "If I didn't know better, I'd think you're hoping this sting is unsuccessful," he said.

"Well, we all hope that, don't we?" asked Lucy. "That means that the laws are being obeyed in our town."

"Except for one fact," said Tom. "We know they're not. Since I came here last summer we've arrested thirteen juveniles for operating under the influence."

They looked up as Richie pulled open the door and got in the car. "Mr. Murphy knows me," he said, apologetically. "Maybe

I should have worn a disguise or something."

"That's okay, son," said Scott. "We've got plenty more to try."

But as the evening wore on, Richie continued to be unsuccessful. He wasn't able to buy a single beer. Wherever he tried, in the town's three liquor stores, in the grocery store, even in the roadhouse out near the highway, he was refused.

"Are you sure you're doing exactly what I told you to do?" Tom finally asked him, when he returned empty-handed from the Bilge, a bar down by the waterfront that was a favorite with fishermen.

"Yeah," said Richie. "I just go up to the counter and ask for a Bud. I mean, I don't make any conversation or anything. Should I?"

"Nah," grunted Scott.

"Maybe if I wore my hat," he volunteered, as they pulled up in front of Richard's Fine Wines. He pulled a navy blue watch cap out of his pocket and jammed it down on his head. But the hat didn't fool the clerk, who asked to see his identification. Richie was despondent when he returned to the car. "He offered to sell me a Coke."

"Well, that's it," said Barney, checking his

clipboard. "That was the last one on the list."

"I don't understand it," said Tom, as they drove back to the police station. "I never heard of a liquor sting that didn't net any violators."

"Well, you probably wouldn't," said Lucy. "It's not much of a story if nobody gets caught."

"Are you going to write it up for the paper?" he asked as Barney parked the car.

"Sure. I've spent a lot of time on it already. Besides, Ted likes to print good news whenever he can, especially if it puts his advertisers in a good light."

Tom picked right up on the cue. "It's not often in law enforcement that you have such a satisfying outcome," he said, speaking slowly so she could get every word. "It's gratifying to know that the department's efforts to enforce the legal drinking age are working and that our young people cannot purchase alcohol in Tinker's Cove. And I want to express a special word of thanks to Richie Goodman, who volunteered his time tonight."

Lucy got it all down and climbed out of the car.

"Thanks for inviting me along," she said, shaking Tom's hand. She turned to Richie, who was standing beside her. "Do you have a ride home?"

"Yeah," he said, stuffing his hands in his pockets and striding off toward his car.

"He's a good kid," said Barney, nodding his approval.

"Maybe too good," mused Tom. "Maybe I should have gotten a kid who had more street smarts."

"This is a small town," said Barney. "Everybody knows everybody. The kids probably go a few towns over where nobody knows them. Maybe we should try a joint operation with the Gilead P.D."

"It's a thought," admitted Tom. "Or maybe we could just try not to tip off the storekeepers in advance."

Under the lights that illuminated the parking lot Lucy could see Barney's face redden. "Nothing like that happened," he said.

"If you say so," said Scott, replacing his cap on his head and marching into the building.

"Barney, you didn't do anything like that, did you?" asked Lucy, as she watched the lieutenant stride off.

"No, damn it, but I was sure tempted. I don't like this kind of stuff. It's awful close to entrapment, if you ask me. I'd rather wait for somebody to commit a crime, and then arrest them. I don't like to trick 'em into it."

"Police do undercover operations all the time. It's perfectly legal."

"Well, that don't make it right." Barney planted his cap on his head and shifted his belt. "You know what he wants me to do now? I'm supposed to put a box out on the desk when I visit the schools and tell the kids they can write me a note about anything that's bothering them. Like maybe if their big brother is smoking pot or something like that. And I'm supposed to tell the kids it's just between them and me and nobody will get in trouble. But that's not true. The lootenant here wants me to pass on suspected violations to the school authorities, and by law, they have to report drug use to the police."

"Do people know about this? Maybe I should write a story."

"Oh, I wouldn't do that if I were you," said Barney, waggling his finger at her. "Your daughter has come to the attention of the department — you wouldn't want her investigated, now, would you?"

"Tom said everything was okay, that he was dropping the whole thing."

"And he will," said Barney, giving her a wink, "as long as you do things his way."

■ ■ ■ ■

Barney was way off base, thought Lucy, as she drove home. She had Tom's word that he wasn't going to investigate the inhaler incident any further. There was nothing to investigate, for that matter. There was no law against helping a person in distress, Tom had said so himself. He'd said Elizabeth should be congratulated for her quick thinking.

Poor Barney was under a lot of stress. He was no doubt worried sick about Marge. This was no time for him to have to adjust to a whole new way of doing things at work. After all, Barney had been on the force for twenty years or more, working the whole time for Chief Crowley. It was no wonder he was having trouble accepting the lieutenant's ideas about community policing.

But even Barney had admitted that the lieutenant was getting results — hadn't he bragged to her about the department's success in preserving the evidence that nailed Steve Cummings?

The lieutenant certainly seemed to know what he was doing, thought Lucy, as she turned onto Red Top Road. And he was truly committed to his job. She remembered how his voice had cracked with emotion when he described finding the young couple dead in the crash, how he couldn't forget the flowers on the girl's wrist. White roses.

What a tragedy, she thought, blinking back tears. And it would make a great lead when she wrote about the sting for *The Pennysaver.* She pulled into her driveway and braked, turning off the ignition. This was one story she couldn't wait to write.

CHAPTER THIRTEEN

6 days 'til Xmas

"Great story, Lucy," said Ted, after he finished reading her report on the sting operation.

Lucy had been so eager to write it that she'd gone into *The Pennysaver* office first thing Friday morning, way ahead of deadline.

"You don't think I went over the top?"

When she had been writing the story, Lucy had been carried along in a rush of creative energy. Now that it was finished, she was beginning to have second thoughts. Maybe she should have taken the time to make a few phone calls to New York to check the accuracy of Scott's account.

"No. Great detail, especially the white roses."

Lucy felt better; Ted was a lot more experienced in the news business than she was.

"Our advertisers will love it," he continued. "Good news for once."

"I knew you'd say that." Lucy took a deep breath and plunged in. "Do you think maybe we're getting a bit too concerned about the advertisers? I mean, it seems to come up an awful lot lately."

"Damn right it does. Adam wants to go to BU — do you know how much that costs? Frankly, this paper makes a pretty thin profit as it is, and I can't afford to alienate any advertisers right now. Not if Adam's going to get a college education."

"You'll get financial aid."

"Not enough — I've done the calculations. And a lot of that aid is probably going to be student loans, which I'd like to avoid if I can. I don't want Adam starting out with a huge debt burden."

"That worries me, too," admitted Lucy.

"The good news is that revenues are ahead of budget this month thanks to that new Ropewalk mall. They've placed a lot of holiday advertising with us."

"That's great," said Lucy. "Ho, ho, ho!" She shrugged into her coat and buttoned it up. "I'll see you Monday."

In the car, she turned on the radio. The local station was also getting plenty of ads; as she drove she heard commercials urging her to celebrate the holiday season in a variety of ways: with specially decorated Dunkin' Donuts packed in festive jars, with a new car from Fat Eddie and his "happy, holiday elves" who were practically giving away the new models in a burst of Christmas spirit, and with a "luxurious," meaning expensive, outfit from the Carriage Trade. And if the stress of the season was getting her down, a public service announcement informed her she could call the Samaritans for counseling.

If she were honest with herself, she thought, it did seem as if a gray cloud of depression was following her wherever she went these days. It was partly a reaction to the forced jollity of the Christmas season, but she was also struggling to cope with Tucker's murder and Steve's arrest. And if that weren't enough, she was anxious about the kids: Toby's experiments with pot and his lackadaisical attitude about the college applications, not to mention Elizabeth's suspension. This was not the Christmas she had hoped for.

She had intended to stop by at Miss Tilley's to deliver a Christmas present, but in her present mood she wasn't sure it was a good idea. When she got to the corner of

Miss Tilley's road, however, she found herself flipping on the turn signal and accelerating. Through the years she had found there was nothing like a conversation with Miss Tilley to put things in their proper perspective.

Julia Ward Howe Tilley, who allowed only a sadly diminished number of contemporaries to call her by her first name, was the first person who befriended Lucy when she and Bill had moved to Tinker's Cove. Then the librarian at the Broadbrooks Free Library, Miss Tilley had noticed Lucy's interest in mysteries and began saving the new titles for her. As they grew to know each other, Lucy had come to appreciate Miss Tilley's tart wit and no-nonsense attitude. Now that she was retired and steadily growing frailer, Lucy tried to stop by for a chat as often as she could.

Rachel Goodman opened the door when Lucy knocked. After her auto accident a few years ago, Miss Tilley arranged to have Rachel help her with meals, housekeeping, and driving.

"Hi, Rachel," said Lucy, as she took off her coat. "You'll be reading about your son in the paper next week."

"Nothing bad I hope," said Rachel, hanging it up in the coat closet.

"No. You should be proud. He did a great job on that liquor sting."

Rachel grimaced. "He didn't want to do it, but he didn't feel as if he could refuse. Richie thought that if he said no, the lieutenant would think he was in the habit of buying booze illegally."

It occured to Lucy that both Stones, Steffie and Tom, definitely had the knack of putting people on the spot.

"Come to think of it, he did seem a little uncomfortable, but I figured it was just part of being seventeen."

Rachel shook her head. "No. He didn't like the idea of tricking people and getting them in trouble. Plus, he does have a bit of a guilty conscience, I think. Now that he's got his acceptance from Harvard, he's come down with a wicked case of senioritis. He's been spending a lot of time with Tim Rogers, and I don't think they're memorizing Bible verses." She lowered her voice to a whisper. "Frankly, I don't know why the police are so concerned about underage drinking — the real problem at the high school is drugs, if you ask me."

Lucy would have loved to share her own thoughts on this subject, but was interrupted.

"Who are you talking to?" Miss Tilley asked in a quavery voice from the next room. "I thought I heard Lucy Stone."

Lucy went into the living room, where Miss Tilley was seated in an antique Boston rocker next to the fireplace, with a bright crocheted afghan across her knees. A small fire was burning on the hearth. Lucy gave her old friend a quick peck on the cheek and presented her with a foil package wrapped with a bright red bow.

"What is this?"

"Scottish shortbread. Elizabeth made it."

"What a clever girl."

"Not that clever, I'm afraid," said Lucy, seating herself on the camelback sofa. "She's been suspended from school."

"I can't believe it," said Rachel.

"It's true," said Lucy, telling them the whole story. When she had finished, Miss Tilley clucked her tongue.

"Zero tolerance sounds like a good policy for people who have zero common sense and zero intelligence. You tell Elizabeth she did the right thing, and she shouldn't hesitate to do it again. Goodness sakes, rules are made to be broken."

Lucy chuckled. "It's nice to hear you say that. I was beginning to have doubts myself."

"But what about school?" asked Rachel. "Two weeks is a long time. Won't she miss a lot of classwork?"

"Toby gets her assignments for her and she's been keeping up at home. It's kind of nice having her around the house, actually. She's been doing a lot of baking and has started making herself a dress to wear on Christmas."

Rachel shook her head. "It seems like she got a rum deal to me. I'll ask Bob to give Mr. Humphreys a call. He's been known to become a bit more tolerant when he's faced with legal action. The school committee hates to pay legal bills." She stood up. "How about some tea to go with that shortbread?"

When Rachel had gone into the kitchen, Miss Tilley leaned forward and tapped Lucy's knee with her bony hand.

"Elizabeth's not the only one who's being treated unfairly — what do you think about poor Dr. Cummings?"

Lucy shrugged. "Lee asked me to see if I could find out anything, and I talked to Barney — he says it's pretty much an open-and-shut case. They're certain he did it."

"Nonsense. Steve Cummings has been taking care of my teeth for years. . . ." She pulled back her lips and tapped her yellowed incisors. "I still have all my own teeth,

I'll have you know, and that's thanks to Dr. Cummings. I ask you, do you really think a man who has the patience to put up with an old horror like me would even think of committing murder? It's just not in him. He's a kind, good man."

"You only know him professionally," argued Lucy. "He's no saint. He left Lee and the girls and he was dating Tucker, who was only half his age. Isn't it possible the situation got out of hand, and he lost control and killed her?"

"This doesn't much sound like the Lucy Stone I know," observed Miss Tilley, taking a cup and saucer from Rachel. "What's happened to that inquisitive mind of yours? Since when did you start swallowing the official line?"

Stung, Lucy took a consoling sip of tea. Miss Tilley sure had a way of getting right to the heart of the matter. Wishing she knew the answer, she delayed by taking a bite of shortbread.

"When it seems the only logical conclusion," she finally said, but she had the uneasy feeling that Miss Tilley was right. Lately, it seemed to her, she'd been spending a lot of energy avoiding facts that didn't fit rather than trying to work out the truth for herself.

"Actually," she found herself saying, "I do have another theory about Tucker's murder — but it's so awful I haven't even been able to think about it."

"What is it?" asked Rachel. Both she and Miss Tilley were leaning forward in their chairs, eager to hear.

"Well, I found Tucker's agenda — it had been missing. It turned out it was jammed behind a drawer in her desk at the day-care center. There wasn't much in it, but there was a notation the Sunday before she died. Apparently she'd had a meeting with Lee."

"You think Lee killed her?" Rachel's hand flew to her mouth. "I can't believe it. Besides, that was Sunday. Tucker wasn't killed until Wednesday morning."

"What if Lee met with Tucker on Sunday and begged her to give up Steve and Tucker refused," argued Lucy. "That would give Lee a strong motive to kill her, wouldn't it? She was desperate to get back with Steve. You saw how she treated Tucker at the cookie exchange."

Rachel bit her lip.

"The female of the species is more deadly than the male." Miss Tilley nodded with satisfaction. "I knew it couldn't be Dr. Cummings."

"It can't be Lee, either." Rachel shook her

head. "Think of those two little girls. What would happen to them?"

"I know," agreed Lucy. "Hillary and Gloria. That's why I don't even want to think about it."

"Their father could take care of them if she went to jail." Miss Tilley snapped off a piece of shortbread and popped it in her mouth. "I think you should go straight to the police with this information. Where's the agenda now?"

Lucy's and Rachel's eyes met. "It's gone. Sue sent it to Tucker's parents."

"That doesn't matter. The police should consider all the evidence. You have a responsibility to tell them."

Lucy shook her head. "A minute ago you were telling me to think for myself. Well, I don't think anything would be gained by making Lee the subject of an investigation. If Steve is really innocent, well, it will undoubtedly come out at the trial, and he'll be acquitted."

"You'd leave those innocent little girls in the hands of a murderer?" Miss Tilley was shocked.

"Well, if she did murder Tucker, it was only because she was desperate to save her family," said Lucy. "Besides, I don't have any real proof — just a theory. This time

I'm going to mind my own business."

"Let the police earn their salaries, that's what Bob always says," advised Rachel.

"Well," snorted Miss Tilley. "I can only say how glad I am that I remained a single lady. Marriage apparently has a terrible effect on one's morals."

"And it only gets worse when you become a parent," added Lucy darkly.

As she drove home, Lucy listened again to the steady barrage of holiday commercials. She tried to change the station but it didn't make any difference whether she listened to 102.9 or 107.5 or 98.8 — it was all buy, buy, buy. Disgusted, she reached to turn it off, but paused when she heard the familiar strains of one of her favorite carols.

As she sang along, she remembered that the community carol sing was that night. They'd go, she decided, the whole family. It was just what they needed to restore their Christmas spirit.

Much to her surprise, everyone was agreeable when she presented her plan at the dinner table. Sara and Zoe loved any excuse to sing Christmas songs, Elizabeth was tired of being stuck at home, and Toby saw an opportunity to socialize with his friends. Even

Bill agreed to give up an evening of channel surfing.

"There's nothing good on TV on Friday, anyway," he said.

Bill and Lucy took the Subaru, along with the younger girls, while Toby drove the truck, with Elizabeth for company. He hoped to hook up with his friends, in which case he would need his own transportation home.

"Behave yourself," Bill warned, as he handed over the keys.

A light snow was falling when their two-car caravan arrived in town, and Christmas lights were twinkling on most of the houses. A Christmas tree had been placed on the porch roof of the general store, and a bonfire was burning brightly in the parking area out front. A crowd of people had already gathered and were singing, accompanied by Stan Pulaski, the fire chief, on the trumpet.

"We three kings of Orient are . . ." was one of Lucy's favorites and she joined in eagerly. She knew the words by heart, but the kids didn't; somebody passed them a sheaf of paper with the lyrics.

This was what Christmas was really all about, thought Lucy. Neighbors and friends gathered to enjoy old songs, raising their voices together to celebrate the season. She looked from face to face, familiar faces lighted by the glow of the bonfire, and felt a warm sense of fellowship. It was wonderful to be in this place at this moment, she thought, placing her hand in Bill's.

The general store faced the town green, an open space with grass and a few trees that afforded the carolers a clear view of the little town: the main street lined with stores, all decorated with Christmas lights, and beyond, the harbor, where some of the fishing boats had also been trimmed with holiday lights. The restored Ropewalk stood next to the fish pier, its unique shape outlined with strings of twinkling white lights.

Stan had played the first few notes of "Silent Night" when a sudden explosion rocked the ground they were standing on. Everyone looked up, there was a collective intake of breath. Flames were shooting from one of the narrow windows of the Ropewalk.

Lucy saw Stan running toward the firehouse, clutching his trumpet to his chest. A few others, volunteer firemen, also ran to help. Moments later the scream of sirens filled the air as the fire engines roared out of the station and tore off down the street. The rest of the carolers stood rooted in place, watching in horror as the flames grew larger and smoke began to billow into the night sky.

CHAPTER FOURTEEN

Suddenly, they were all running down Main Street toward the fire. Everyone wanted to see the spectacle; it was the biggest thing that had happened since the sardine cannery fire some twenty years ago.

"This is history being made right here," Lucy heard one man tell his son. "You look and don't forget and you'll have something to tell your grandkids."

All Lucy could think about, as she ran along with the crowd, were the people inside the mall. With less than a week left to Christmas it must have been packed with shoppers. She remembered the clutter of stalls and the narrow walkways, not to mention the aged wood. It had all looked most attractive, but Lucy wouldn't have wanted to be inside it in a fire. It wouldn't take much smoke to turn the old building into a death trap.

Holding tight to Zoe's hand, Lucy followed Bill, hurrying to keep up with him. Toby had run ahead with his friends, Elizabeth had also joined a group of high schoolers. Sara ran along with her father.

No one had had time to set up barricades, but the crowd didn't advance past the edge of the Ropewalk parking lot, where the fire trucks were parked and the volunteer firemen were laying hose. There, you could smell the smoke and feel the heat of the flames that had now spread from a single ground-floor window to several more, including some on the second floor. People were streaming from the exits, holding scarves and handkerchiefs to their soot-blackened faces. Lucy spotted Franny and ran up to her, first making sure that Bill had a firm hold on Zoe's hand.

"Are you okay?" she asked.

Franny coughed and nodded in reply.

"Can everybody get out?"

"I think so." Franny dabbed at her eyes. "It's dinnertime, so there weren't too many people, yet. Frank Crowell, he's the manager, raised the alarm and told people to go to the exits. Do you see him?"

Lucy and Franny scanned the faces of the people in the crowd looking for Frank, who was instantly recognizable because of his flamboyant handlebar mustache.

When they failed to see him, Franny began asking who had seen him last.

"He was behind me," said a woman Lucy recognized. She had a stall selling stained-glass suncatchers and lampshades that she made herself. "I heard his voice, telling everyone to keep moving."

"Did he get out?"

"No. I saw him go back," added a tiny woman with curly white hair, who was clutching her Ropewalk shopping bag as if it were a life preserver. "He got us to the exit and then he turned back." She shook her head. "I don't know why."

Hearing this, Franny ran up to Chief Pulaski, who was giving orders through his megaphone. Lucy followed, but couldn't hear what Franny was saying over the din of the sirens and the throb of the pumper truck's diesel engines. She saw Pulaski shake his head, mouthing something to two new arrivals, volunteer firemen who were pulling on their gear. Lucy caught a glimpse of a head of thick red hair just before one of the men put on his helmet.

By now, huge flames were leaping from the Ropewalk windows, bathing everything and everyone in a flickering red light. Now and then there was a popping nose; someone said it was window glass exploding from the heat of the fire. The parking lot was filled with fire trucks, hoses snaked everywhere, and in the distance sirens could be heard as fire companies from the neighboring towns of Gilead, Smithfield, Hopkinton, and Perry answered the call for mutual aid.

Lucy watched as the two firefighters lowered their face shields and vanished into the burning building. The last thing she saw was the reflective letters on the backs of their coats. They had the same name: Rousseau.

"Why aren't they pumping any water yet?" she asked Bill.

"It takes time to lay hose," he said, as water started streaming from two, then three hoses. "Here it comes."

"Finally." Lucy was clutching herself, her arms across her chest. She was holding her breath, waiting for the two Rousseaus to emerge from the building.

They finally did, holding an unconscious figure between them, just as flames began to erupt from the roof and everyone had given them up for lost.

EMTs rushed up with oxygen and a stretcher, and police officers began setting up sawhorse barricades, pushing everyone back to the sidewalk on the opposite side of the street.

Moments after the street had been cleared, a ladder track began moving very slowly along it, stopping so hoses could be shifted to minimize the damage of the heavy truck rolling over them.

"They'll never be able to save it," said Bill, and Lucy realized he was right. The firefighters were now spraying water on neighboring buildings, the harbormaster's office, and a row of shops that included Jake's Donut Shack, a real estate office and a T-shirt shop. "This street's so narrow the buildings are awfully close together," he said. "It'll be a miracle if the whole block doesn't go."

As she watched, Lucy began to make out the faces of people she knew. Rachel's husband, Bob, was one of the volunteer firefighters, so was Hank Orenstein, Juanita's husband. When a ladder was extended from one of the fire trucks to the roof of the Ropewalk, Lucy gasped to see Hank begin climbing it.

"What's he doing?" she asked Bill.

"Trying to vent the fire, I think. He's going to try to break a hole in the roof."

"Oh my God. What if he falls?" Hank and Juanita's daughter Sadie was Zoe's best friend.

"He'll be careful." Bill put an arm around

her shoulder.

"I hope so." Lucy watched as Hank leaned from the ladder and swung his fire ax, she took a breath and choked on the smoke. What must it be like up on that ladder, so close to the fire? She could only imagine the heat.

The street was now running with water, the red-and-yellow flames were reflected in the wet surface. The firefighters' faces were gleaming with sweat, she saw one man lean against an engine, his chest heaving as he mopped his face. An EMT approached him, offering an oxygen mask, and he took it.

All at once, it was too much for Lucy. She couldn't watch anymore. It wasn't just a spectacle, something to see. Real people's lives were going up in smoke. She thought of all the individual craftsmen who had opened shops in the Ropewalk, all the labor they had put into making and marketing their wares. The Ropewalk was supposed to offer a new chance to people in the economically beleaguered town, now all those hopes and dreams were going up in smoke. Lucy turned away.

"I can't watch anymore," she said to Bill.

"Are you going home?" he asked.

It was tempting. Their house was far from the fire. She could take a bath, make herself a snack, even go to bed with a book.

"No." She shook her head, watching as several more firefighters collapsed against the ambulance, waiting for their turn at the oxygen. Down the street, the clean, white light from the IGA's plate-glass windows caught her eye.

"I'm going to get some food and drink for the men — they need nourishment and fluids," she said.

Bill nodded and hoisted Zoe up onto his shoulders, where she perched like a little monkey. Lucy hurried down the street, relieved to get away from the overwhelming sights and sounds of the fire.

When she approached the store, she saw the cashier, Dot Kirwan, standing in the doorway, arms folded across her chest, watching from a distance.

"That's a real shame, that is," she said, nodding grimly.

"All that work, all those high hopes," agreed Lucy.

"Don't tell me you're doing your Friday night grocery shopping," said Dot. "I haven't had a customer since the sirens went off."

"I thought I'd get some juice and stuff for the men — they've been at this for quite a while and they look like they need to refuel."

"Why didn't I think of that?" Dot grabbed a cart and pushed it over to the dairy case where she started filling it with gallon jugs of fruit punch and cartons of orange juice.

Lucy took another cart and wheeled it to the bakery aisle, where she grabbed boxes of doughnuts and loaves of bread. A few aisles over she found big jars of peanut butter and jelly and added them.

"Ring this all up — I'll use my charge card, OK?"

"I don't think so," said Dot, raising her eyebrows. "Joe can take it off his taxes as a charitable donation." Joe Marzetti was the owner, but Dot really ran the store. "I'll just get a knife or two and we'll be off." She hurried over to the deli counter and grabbed some sandwich spreaders; as an afterthought she grabbed a package of paper cups.

Pushing the cart back down the street toward the burning Ropewalk, Lucy felt better. At least she was making herself useful. The policeman at the barricade pushed the sawhorse aside when he saw them coming and they rolled their carts next to the ambulance. Dot passed out the juice while Lucy made sandwiches, using the child seat of the cart as a work surface.

Up close, she saw the toll the fire was taking on the firefighters. One man's helmet rolled onto the ground and she bent to pick it up, shocked to discover how heavy it was as she handed it back to him. Underneath their heavy slickers the men were sweating, and their faces were blackened with soot. Just walking in their heavy rubber boots and coats had to be an effort, and many of the men were also burdened with tanks of air. Yet they scrambled up the ladders and hauled hoses around, never hesitating when they were given an order.

"I hate it when there are fires down here," said one tired firefighter. "The whole town could go up."

"We're earning our pay tonight," said another, tilting back his head and gulping down a quart of orange juice.

"How much do you make?" asked Lucy, handing him a sandwich.

"A hundred and fifty dollars a year," he said, with his mouth full of peanut butter. "We're basically volunteers. One of the last volunteer companies in the state."

"You're doing an amazing job," said Lucy. "Who were those guys who went into the building?"

"That was Rusty and J.J. — disobeying the chief, like usual."

"It's gonna go — all clear!" she heard

someone yell and looked up. The hose crews began moving back, individual firefighters ran for safety as the huge front wall of the building began to fall. There was a huge crash and a spray of glowing red cinders rose and fell, showering those closest to the blaze.

The firefighters moved back in, pouring water onto the remains of the building. Nothing was left of the Ropewalk but a smoldering heap. Some of the fire companies began to pack up their equipment, preparing to leave.

Surveying the scene Lucy was struck by the unfamiliar new shape of the waterfront, the space formerly occupied by the Ropewalk was now vacant, revealing a view of the harbor beyond. The neighboring buildings had all been saved, but it would have to wait until morning to learn if they had been damaged.

Ted approached her. "Can a reporter have a sandwich?"

"Sure," said Lucy, spreading peanut butter on a piece of bread for him. "Some story."

"Not the kind I like to write," said Ted, taking a big bite of his sandwich.

"Do they know how it started?"

"Not yet."

"Any word about the manager, Frank Crowell?"

He shook his head.

She turned away. She'd had enough, she was bone tired, she wanted to go home.

"Lucy, can I help?" It was Franny.

Lucy remembered how proud Franny had been of her jewelry shop in the Ropewalk, how excited she'd been about having her own business. "I'm so sorry for you," she said, enfolding her in a hug.

Franny shrugged. "I was pretty lucky. I hadn't moved my workshop into the Ropewalk, yet. All my supplies and equipment are still at home. All I had there were finished pieces, and frankly, I'd sold most of them. I didn't lose much at all." She blinked a few times. "Most of the others weren't so fortunate. I don't know what they're going to do. They've lost everything, and they're going to have to start over from scratch." She paused a moment. "If they can."

Lucy nodded. "Well, Dot should be back soon. She went to make some coffee for the guys who'll be here all night."

"Here you go," said Franny, slapping a sandwich together for a very small firefighter from a neighboring town. The firefighter yanked off his helmet and two braids tumbled down; Lucy realized he wasn't a he at all.

More power to her thought Lucy, as she said good-bye to Franny and rejoined Bill and the girls. Not, of course, that she'd want her girls to become firefighters. The work was too hard and too dangerous. Then she remembered Tucker. Nothing was safe, it seemed.

"Let's go home," she said, wrapping her arms around Bill and resting her cheek on his chest.

He gave her a squeeze. "You bet."

CHAPTER FIFTEEN

5 days 'til Xmas

Lucy was headed out the door on Saturday morning to do her grocery shopping when the phone rang. It was Ted with an assignment.

"The volunteer firefighters are meeting on Monday night — can you cover it?"

"Sure." Lucy checked her calendar and wrote in the time of the meeting. "Are they handing out awards or something? Should I take my camera?"

Ted snorted. "Definitely take your camera, but it's not about awards. Several firefighters have been charged with stealing from the fire. The meeting is to decide what the organization is going to do — they might go on strike in protest."

"Whoa." Lucy couldn't believe what she was hearing. "This is the first I've heard about this. Explain."

"Can't. I don't have time. I've got to be at

a press conference in five minutes. Stop by the office later today, OK?"

"OK."

She had almost made it to the door when the phone rang a second time. This time it was Mr. Humphreys from the high school.

"Ahem, Mrs. Stone," he began, clearing his throat several times.

Whatever he had to say was apparently stuck in his craw. Finally, he managed to get it out.

"I had a conversation with your legal representative yesterday, and I think I may say it was most enlightening and informative. As a result of that conversation, Elizabeth's suspension has been reduced and she will be welcome to return to school on Monday."

Lucy resisted the impulse to crow. "That's very good news," she said. "Thank you for calling."

In the car, she flipped on the radio just in time to hear the nine o'clock news report. Ted was right. Four volunteer firemen had been arrested and would be charged with larceny at the Ropewalk fire: Russell Rousseau, Jean-Jacques Rousseau, Fred Childs, and George Paxton. Paxton was also the captain of the volunteer force, next in line of command after the chief, Stan Pulaski. All four men had been released on bail pending their arraignment Monday. Tinker's Cove police were expected to release more details later this morning.

The station promised a "six-pack" — six songs without a commercial — but Lucy couldn't have told you what they were. She was hardly listening; her mind was occupied by this disturbing news.

Last night she had been at the fire and witnessed firsthand the heroism of the volunteer firefighters, especially the Rousseau brothers. Everyone in town understood the risks involved in fighting fires, and Tinker's Cove citizens were proud of the volunteer firefighters. The force was one of the last volunteer departments in the state. Most of the neighboring towns had been forced to switch to paid, professional forces, but interest in Tinker's Cove remained high and the chief was never short of volunteers. Members of the department marched in the Fourth of July parade; afterward they held a huge picnic and invited the whole town to watch as they competed in contests of skill such as ladder races and obstacle courses. The most popular, especially if the weather was hot, was to see who could hit a target with water from the fire hose. It was funny to watch people struggle with the hose, which seemed to have a life of its own. Kids and women were usually knocked off their feet; only the strongest men could control the jet of water that shot out of it.

Why would such public-spirited men as the volunteer firefighters steal from a fire? She'd never heard of such a thing, but she could understand them taking souvenirs like a sign, perhaps a brick or a unique bit of woodwork. It would be something to keep, a reminder of the night the Ropewalk burned. But that could hardly be called theft, she thought, except by the strictest moralist.

Lucy knew that many people in Tinker's Cove had been seafarers for generations, and weren't above picking up a loose bit of flotsom or jetsam and claiming it for their own. When she and Bill were first married they had found a wooden cable spool washed up on a beach and rolled it home, where they had used it as a table for years. Most anything that washed up was considered free for the taking, except for lobster traps. They were left for their owner to reclaim; you could get shot for taking somebody else's lobster trap.

Turning onto Main Street, Lucy gasped at the sight of the burned Ropewalk. Nothing of the building remained except for a huge heap of burned wood; the paint on the neighboring block of stores had blistered, and the roof shingles had curled with the heat. It was amazing that the firefighters had been able to save the stores — even the church across the street was black with soot. The street in front of the Ropewalk had been closed off with yellow tape; water used to fight the fire had frozen overnight, making it too slippery for traffic.

Lucy took the detour, straining her neck to get a last look as she made the turn and headed for the IGA.

While she waited in line at the checkout, she listened to Dot chatting with the woman ahead of her.

"It doesn't surprise me in the least bit," said Dot, as she passed the cans and boxes through the scanner. "My oldest boy, he was on the Tinker's Cove force for years but then he went professional over in Gilead. He's an EMT and all; he got trained when he was in the army.

"Well, Joe told me, one of the reasons he wanted to go pro was that he didn't like some of the stuff the volunteers were doing." She paused to find the UPC code on a box of cat food. "I swear, sometimes they hide these darn things. Anyway, Joe said, the attitude was that they could take whatever they wanted because the insurance company would be paying for it all anyway." Dot's eyebrows shot up. "And I told him that was a lot of poppy-cock because we'd all end up paying higher insurance rates. There's no such thing as a free lunch, that's what I told him."

Soon Dot had the woman's groceries bagged, and she turned to Lucy.

"Seems like I'm seeing an awful lot of you," she said.

"I can't seem to stay away," agreed Lucy, with a smile. "Last night was quite a night, wasn't it?"

"One I wouldn't care to repeat, thank you," said Dot, reaching for a bag of apples and smoothing the plastic so the scanner could read the price code.

"Last night I thought those men were heroes, and today I hear on the radio that they're bums — I can't figure it out," Lucy said.

"In my experience, most men are a little bit of both, if you know what I mean." Dot leaned across the counter. "But I can tell you this much. If Chief Crowley was running things down at that police station, this would have been taken care of, and nobody would have been the wiser."

"What do you mean?"

Dot shrugged. "He mostly turned a blind eye, figuring that the firemen deserved whatever they could salvage — it isn't like they get paid or anything. If somebody complained or something, he would have them return the stuff. It all would have been taken care of without making people look bad."

"That's true," chimed in Andrea Rogers, who had stepped up to the checkout behind Lucy. "Chief Crowley would never have brought charges against Tim. He would have given him a talking-to and brought him home, figuring his parents would take care of it. Now they're got this zero tolerance policy." Andrea twisted her lips into a smirk. "It's supposed to be zero tolerance for drugs and booze, but I think it really means zero tolerance for kids."

Lucy nodded in agreement; she was a sadder and wiser woman after Elizabeth's experience.

"I think you've got something there. Has Tim gone to court yet?"

"Not 'til January. Bob says they'll probably put him on probation and make him take an alcohol education course, plus he'll be stuck with a conviction." Andrea sighed.

"Every time he applies for a job or renews his driver's license or whatever, he'll have to check the yes box."

"Look on the bright side," said Lucy. "The way things are going, he'll have plenty of company. What about next year?"

"MCU doesn't want him anymore, that's for sure. We're thinking of sending him for a thirteenth year at Wolford Academy. He can play there and hopefully he'll get recruited by another college."

"That's a good idea," said Lucy, watching as Dot rang up the last of her order.

"That'll be one fifty-four and thirty-one cents."

"Ouch," said Lucy, reaching for her wallet.

At *The Pennysaver,* Lucy found Ted hunched over his desk, tapping away at his keyboard. She plopped down in the chair he saved for visitors, not bothering to move the clutter of press releases that had accumulated there.

"Listen, Ted. I'm not sure this firefighter story rates page one. From what I heard at the IGA this morning, this is nothing new. The firemen have taken stuff in the past, and Chief Crowley just turned a blind eye on it unless he got a complaint. Then he'd make them return the stuff, but he didn't bring charges or anything. Tom Scott's new on the job; he doesn't understand about small towns."

Ted looked up and Lucy saw he looked like someone who hadn't been getting enough sleep. She also thought he looked terribly sad, showing none of the excitement he usually felt when working on a big story.

"I hate this story," he confessed. "These men risk their lives, they get up out of warm beds in the middle of the night to put out fires and pry people out of crashed cars, and they don't get paid a penny. Do I care if they take some souvenirs from a fire? Do I care if they help themselves to some fire-damaged stuff that's going to get thrown out anyway? I don't give a damn, and that's the truth. But I've got to cover it because it's already been on the radio and Tom Scott held a big news conference this morning and invited media from all over New England. Goddamn *Globe* was there."

He dropped his hands in his lap and shook his head. "What really gets me is that I'm the only one who's going to mention what this is really about — and only a few thousand people are going to read me and hundreds of thousands are going to read the story Scott's hand-fed to everybody else. It was slick, let me tell you. Piles of merchandise, stacked up on tables, for all to view. Gold and silver jewelry. Rare coins. Everything all polished up. Even a couple of stained-glass lamps. Worth thousands of dollars, or so he said."

"I had no idea. I thought it was a couple of bricks or something like that."

"Nope. You gotta hand it to the boys. They made quite a haul. But that's not the story, not really. Because it wasn't the shopkeepers who complained — I've been calling them, and they have nothing but good things to say about the firefighters. They all say their businesses were total losses anyway. Nope. You know who filed the complaint. The Gilead fire chief."

Lucy was beginning to understand. "And Gilead is a professional force."

"Right. And they're asking for a raise at the town meeting this year. . . ."

"And they don't want to have to explain why folks in Gilead have to pay for something folks in Tinker's Cove get for free," interjected Lucy.

Ted nodded. "And if the volunteers go on strike, which is what they're threatening to do, they'll look even worse, and the voters will get disgusted. This is the end of the volunteers, I'm telling you. When this is over, Tinker's Cove will have a professional fire department. It's the end of an era."

He paused, studying his hands, then raised his head.

"Thanks for covering the meeting for me. I hated to ask, but the kids' Christmas concert is Monday night, and Pam says I have to go."

"No problem," said Lucy.

CHAPTER SIXTEEN

3 days 'til Xmas

As soon as Lucy opened the door to the fire station she heard the rumble of the men's voices. She nodded at the dispatcher and went past his desk into the common room, where CPR classes and training sessions were held. The last time Lucy had been there was when she covered the rabies clinic last spring; then the big room had been filled with assorted dogs and cats, and their owners and the conversation had been friendly as people chatted about their pets.

Tonight, the mood was much different. The gathered firefighters were angry and sullen. Lucy could feel the tension when she entered the room, and it made her pause. The only thing that kept her from turning and fleeing was the knowledge that Ted was counting on her to cover the meeting.

Heads turned and people stared at her;

someone snickered and she realized she was the only woman in the room. Dot had been right on the mark when she said the Tinker's Cove Volunteer Fire Department was a men's club. "She writes for the paper," she heard someone say, and the word was passed through the room. Lucy felt uncomfortable under the gaze of so many men and looked for a familiar face. She was relieved when she spotted Bob Goodman, Rachel's husband, and Hank Orenstein sitting in the back. There were empty chairs next to them so she approached them.

"Hi, Lucy," Bob said with a smile. "Sit yourself down."

Bob was a tall, lean man with wire-rimmed glasses. He was the only man in the room who was wearing a suit.

"Thanks. For a minute there I felt a bit unwelcome. This doesn't seem like a very friendly group. And thanks for calling Mr. Humphreys. Elizabeth went back to school today."

Bob nodded. For a lawyer, he was remarkably taciturn.

Raised voices and the crash of a chair falling caught their attention, and Lucy glanced nervously around the room.

"Are these guys always so rowdy?" she asked.

"They're not so bad when you get to know them," said Hank. "They're just a little upset."

Hank was shorter and heavier than Bob, with a round face and a beard. He ran a co-operative that sold heating oil and energy-saving devices at discount prices.

"Do you think they'll really strike?" asked Lucy.

"Might," said Bob.

"A lot of them want to," said Hank. "At least the ones I talked to today. They feel like those boys are getting a raw deal."

"Ted says it was an awful lot of stuff — worth thousands of dollars." Lucy kept her voice low; she didn't want to be overheard.

Hank snorted in disgust. "Those boys were just plain greedy."

Bob nodded. "This time they went too far."

"What do you mean?"

The two men exchanged a glance, then Hank broke the silence.

"So, how's Bill doing? Is he keepin' busy this winter?"

"Bill's fine. And you don't have to worry that I'm going to quote you in the paper. Anything you say is off the record. Promise. But I sure could use some background information, and from what you were saying and from what I've been hearing around town it seems like there's been an unofficial policy that it's okay to salvage stuff from fires. Is that true?"

Hank bent closer to Lucy and spoke very softly. "Yeah. I'd say that's true. The boys only get a small stipend — a hundred fifty dollars a year cause it's a volunteer force. And you know what the economy's like in this town. And now with the lobster quota, well, a lot of the guys are really hurting. If they see something they can use, or sell, they're not going to walk away from it. Chief shoulda put a stop to it a long time ago, if you ask me. At first, they didn't take much, but when he never said anything it started to escalate. It's really gotten out of hand."

"So you think Tom Scott did the right thing?"

"Now I didn't say that." Hank's face reddened. "It could have been handled differently. There was no cause to put those boys in jail overnight."

"It wasn't necessary," added Bob. "They all have families in this town; they weren't going to go anywhere."

Lucy nodded, aware that the meeting was beginning. A huge man, still wearing his bright yellow fisherman's waterproof pants pulled up over a ragged sweatshirt and a plaid flannel shirt, was banging on a table with a gavel, calling the meeting to order.

"Quiet down," he roared, his droopy mustache and the bristly whiskers on his chin making him look a little bit like a walrus. "None of us wants to be here all night, so let's get started."

"Who's that?" asked Lucy.

"Claw Rousseau — he owns the lobster pound out on Cove Road," whispered Hank.

"That's the same name as two of the men who were arrested. . . ."

"His sons, Rusty and J.J."

"And he's president of the volunteers' association?"

Hank nodded, and Lucy wrote it all down in her notebook. This could get interesting, she thought.

"This meeting has been called at the request of some of the members," said Claw. "In fact, I have here a petition signed by more than two-thirds of the members calling for the department to go on strike until criminal charges against four of our members have been dropped."

"I move we strike," called out a voice. "Let's vote and get this over with. The Pats are playing Dallas tonight."

This was greeted with raucous laughter.

"Hold your horses," said Claw. "We gotta do this by the rules. First, we gotta have discussion. Who wants to go first?"

Before Claw Rousseau could choose one of the men who had raised his hands, a middle-aged man with a white beard got to his feet and took the floor.

"This isn't right," he began. "What the hell's going on in this town? Here we have four fine young men, willing to risk their lives in order to help other folks, being treated as if they were common criminals. What we have here is a crime all right, but the crime isn't what Lootenant Scott thinks it is. The crime is taking our good men, they hadn't even had a chance to get out of their gear, and throwing them into jail. That's the crime, and we've gotta let them know that we're not gonna take it. You can't throw us in jail and then expect us to come runnin' to save your ass when you've drove into a 'lectric light pole or put a pot on to cook and forgot all about it and all of a sudden the place is goin' up in smoke. Ain't gonna happen."

The men cheered and stamped their feet in approval, and several jumped to their feet to speak.

"Who was that?" asked Lucy.

"Mike O'Laughlin," said Hank. "He's

always got something to say."

"Got a big mouth," added Bob, leaning back in his chair and crossing his arms on his chest. He seemed to be enjoying himself.

"He's right!" said a thirtyish man in jeans and work boots. "I say we strike 'til the charges are dropped. Let those guys in Gilead cover for us — make 'em earn their fat salaries for a change."

The crowd greeted this with hoots of approval.

"A strike's the only thing that'll teach 'em," said another.

Lucy recognized Gary from the gas station, where he worked as a mechanic.

"I mean, we drop everything when that siren blows, we never hesitate for even a second and we never know what we're gonna face. Last year, Jack Perry and Bill Higgins went to the hospital. Jack had burns and Bill broke his ankle. What do they get for their pain? A big fat nothing. Don't get me wrong. We're all volunteers here, and that's the way it oughta be. People helpin' people. But don't we deserve a little appreciation? A little consideration? That's all we're asking for, and we're gonna get it or they're not gonna get their calls answered."

This also was met with noisy approval. But when Claw recognized Stan Pulaski, the fire chief, the crowd fell silent. Lucy could almost feel the men bristling as he began speaking.

"I know how upset you all are," he began, "and I know how proud you all are to be a volunteer force. But if we go on strike, how are people supposed to have confidence in us? They'll say you can't depend on a volunteer force, and next thing you know we'll be a call force taking orders from a bunch of college-educated strangers who're getting paid to tell us what to do. I think a strike's a bad idea."

"The chief is right," said Claw. He spoke slowly, and his words had weight. "The people of this town have faith in us, that we will answer their calls for help. They trust us and depend on us; we can't let them down."

A sullen silence followed his words. A few of the men looked a bit ashamed of themselves; others were clearly angered.

"Whatsa matter, Chief?" demanded one young man. "What happened to sticking together, like you always say? We gotta work together, isn't that what you're always telling us. Well, we gotta stick behind Rusty and J.J. and the others."

Lucy followed his pointing finger and recognized the two brothers, sitting along with two others who she assumed were the other men who had been charged with stealing. They shifted uneasily in their seats as their fellow firefighters cheered and applauded. After giving vent to their emotions for several minutes, the men quieted down and a single voice was heard.

"Those men broke the law." It was Tom Scott, speaking from the doorway.

His entrance wasn't greated with boos, as Lucy expected. Instead, the men seemed subdued, like a classroom of kids who had lost control when their teacher left the room only to scurry back to their desks when she returned. He strode to the front of the room, where he stood next to Claw Rousseau.

"I know you're angry about the arrests," he began, holding his official blue hat in his hands. "Maybe it'll help if I clear some things up. First of all, I want you to understand that nobody in this town is above the law."

This drew some chuckles from the firefighters, but Scott wasn't fazed.

"Second, I want you to understand that I respect what you do. You fellas are willing to put your lives on the line for your neighbors, and that's a fine and noble thing to do.

"Finally, the district attorney has informed me that he is open to a plea bargain in this matter and is prepared to be lenient."

Scott turned to face Claw and extended his hand. Claw hesitated a moment and then grasped it; Scott pulled him close in a bear hug. From the crowd, there were murmurs of approval as well as mutters of discontent. Claw banged his gavel and called the meeting to order once again.

"There's a motion before us," he said. "We've gotta vote. All in favor, that means a strike, raise your hand."

Tom Scott remained beside him, watching as he counted the votes.

"I count nineteen in favor."

Listening closely, Lucy thought she sensed a note of relief in Claw's voice.

"What does it take? Two-thirds?" she asked Bob.

He nodded. "They don't have the votes."

"Opposed?" called Claw. "A no vote means no strike."

Hank and Bob were among those who raised their hands.

"I count sixteen. The motion fails. No strike." Claw disregarded the angry epithets uttered by some of the thwarted strikers. "Any other business?" He banged down the gavel. "Meeting adjourned."

Lucy got to her feet and tried to make her way to the front of the room to get a comment from Claw. He was already engaged in discussion with several of the firefighters, so Lucy turned to Tom Scott instead.

"Are you pleased with the vote?"

Tom thought for a minute, weighing his words. "I think this is the best possible outcome to an unfortunate situation. A few of the firefighters made a mistake, and that's being addressed by my department and the justice system. I think it's to the credit of the volunteers that they understand their responsibility to the town."

"A majority voted to strike," Lucy reminded him. "Do you think there will be friction between your department and the firefighters in the future?"

"There's no room for petty squabbles in this business," said Scott. "We're public servants, and we work together."

Lucy wrote as fast as she could, but when she looked up to ask her next question she saw that Scott had walked away and was approaching the firefighters who had been charged with theft. The crowd of supporters gathered around them dissipated as he drew near.

Lucy watched as the four men huddled around Scott, wishing she dared to attempt to overhear their conversation. Instead, she wove her way through the scattered groups of firefighters and greeted Claw.

"Lucy Stone, from *The Pennysaver.* Do you mind if I take your picture?"

Claw shrugged and Lucy produced her camera. When the flash went off there was a moment of silence, then the buzz of conversation resumed. She snapped the shutter a few more times, then tucked the camera away and pulled out her notebook.

"Are you happy with the vote?"

"Like everybody else, I can go home tonight and know that if I need help, help will be there."

"What about the men who were charged? Two of them are your sons?"

Rousseau's face sagged and Lucy thought he must be older than she had guessed at first, probably closer to sixty than the robust fifty she had noted in her book. "At times like this you have to have faith," he said.

His answer took her by surprise. She had expected him to defend his sons, or at the very least to point out their heroism at the fire.

"Thank you," she said, and put away her notebook. She didn't want to bother this clearly troubled man any further.

CHAPTER SEVENTEEN

Lucy never worried about going out by herself after dark in Tinker's Cove, but tonight she was unpleasantly aware of her vulnerability as she left the fire station and crossed the parking lot to her car. A group of firefighters had followed her out of the building, and although she could hear their gruff voices and heavy footsteps, she couldn't see them without turning her head. She didn't want them to think she was nervous about their presence, so she kept her eyes forward and tightened her grip on the car keys she held ready in her hand.

As soon as she got inside the car she locked the doors, feeling slightly ridiculous as she did so. She rarely bothered with the locks, but tonight she felt uneasy.

She started the car and carefully backed out of her parking space, then drove slowly across the lot to the exit. There she pulled to a stop and looked right and left to make sure the road was clear; she was ready to pull out when her eyes were suddenly hit with a bright glare. A pickup truck had pulled up behind her and its headlights were set so high that they beamed straight into her mirrors and the bright light bounced directly into her eyes. She squinted, trying to avoid the glare and pulled out. She actually never saw the oncoming car; only the blare of the horn and the screech of brakes as it swerved into the opposite lane to avoid a collision gave her any indication of the danger she had been in.

Her heart was pounding and her hands were shaking as she proceeded slowly down the road. The truck was still close behind her, and the glare was so strong that she was practically blinded, even after she flipped the rearview mirror. She considered pulling over and letting the truck pass, but she knew that probably wasn't a good idea. After all, they were in a passing zone, and there was little traffic. There was no reason why the driver of the truck couldn't pass her if he wanted to. Lucy suspected he was harassing her on purpose and was afraid that if she stopped, he, whoever he was, would pull up right behind her and she would be at his mercy. She didn't really have any choice but to keep going, hoping that her tormenter would eventually grow impatient with her slow speed.

After following her for a mile or so, that's exactly what happened. She heard a roar as the truck accelerated, then zoomed past and raced off down the road. A glance in the rearview mirror explained everything — a police cruiser had apparently scared off her pursuer and was now following her.

She didn't know whether to be relieved or worried, expecting any moment that the blue lights would flash, signalling that she should pull over. That didn't happen, however, and it was only a few moments later that she made the familiar turn onto Red Top Road and finally reached her own driveway; the cruiser paused at the edge of the road and waited until she was safely inside the house before pulling away.

Secure in her kitchen, Lucy let out a sigh of relief as she unzipped her parka and hung it among the other coats and jackets that crowded the row of hooks beside the door. She missed its warmth — Bill had turned down the heat before going up to bed and the kitchen was chilly — and rubbed her arms briskly. Realizing she was too keyed up to go to sleep, she poured a mug of milk for herself and set it in the microwave to heat. She stood, watching the seconds count down, and tried to sort out her emotions.

She should have felt grateful for the police escort, she supposed. It was most likely Tom Scott in the cruiser, she thought. He had probably seen the men following her after the meeting and had decided to keep an eye on the situation. Thanks to his intervention the firefighters had stopped harassing her and she had gotten home safely. He had saved her from goodness knows what unpleasantness, and she owed him a big debt of gratitude.

The microwave beeped, and she took out the milk and sat down at the table, wrapping her hands around the warm mug. Any proper person would be dashing off a thankyou note, she thought, but she didn't feel grateful at all. She was angry, she realized. She was furious that she had needed protection and even madder that Scott had presumed to provide it.

She had lived in this town for nearly twenty years and had managed to get along without police protection until now, and she wasn't sure she had really needed it tonight. Her followers had probably just been teasing her; maybe they hadn't even realized the blinding effect of the truck's headlights.

After all, Tinker's Cove was the sort of place where people never locked their houses. Nobody bothered to lock a car, either, and lots of people even left their keys in the ignition when they parked on Main Street. There were occasional crimes of violence, like Tucker's murder, but they were usually the consequence of emotions gone awry, intimate relationships poisoned by jealousy or alcohol or unemployment, not street crimes like you'd expect in a big city.

It was odd, she thought, that she had never felt the least bit unsafe in Tinker's Cove until now. When Chief Crowley was in charge, the letter of the law had been taken rather lightly, but somehow it had worked, or at least it seemed to.

Now, the attitude was zero tolerance. There were no excuses, no exceptions. It didn't matter if you were an honor student helping another student or a kid supplying drugs to your classmates, you were treated the same. And firefighters who had risked their lives were treated like common criminals. Nowadays nobody winked at a minor transgression, nobody trusted their own judgment, everybody got treated the same.

Except they didn't, realized Lucy, taking a sip of the hot milk and grimacing. It tasted awful. She got up and went into the pantry, looking for some vanilla to flavor it. She didn't find any vanilla but she did find a bottle of brandy she had bought to make eggnog. She poured a dollop in her mug and added a spoonful of sugar. Much better, she decided, as the soothing drink flowed over her tongue.

Zero tolerance might be the official line, she thought, but Mr. Humphreys had backed down soon enough when he had been threatened with legal action. Tom Scott had backed down, too, and offered a plea bargain when the firefighters had threatened to strike.

Lucy finished her drink and set the mug in the sink. Then she stretched, enjoying the sensation of warmth and relaxation the drink had induced. She flipped off the kitchen light and tiptoed up the stairs, ready to go to bed. But when she slipped in beside Bill and closed her eyes, listening to Bill's regular breathing, punctuated by an occasional snore, she couldn't clear her mind for sleep. Disturbing thoughts kept flooding in.

First there was the fire. The huge flames breaking through the Ropewalk roof, the sweaty faces of the firefighters caught in the revolving beams from the emergency lights on top of the trucks. That was how she remembered the fire, but she knew that she didn't have the whole picture. While she had been watching all the activity in the front of the building, something else had been going on in the back, where some of the firefighters had been carrying off valuables. She struggled to reconcile the two images: the brave heroism taking place in the front and the sneaky thievery going on in the back.

Then she saw Claw Rousseau's tired, lined face. Unlike Andrea, he didn't make excuses for his boys or try to defend them. Why not, she wondered. She would have expected Claw to be intensely loyal to his sons. She thought of the panic she felt when she got the call from the high school, and the anger she still nurtured in her heart against Mr. Humphreys. If she felt this strongly about the school's disciplinary policy, why wasn't Claw furious with Scott? Was he really able to set aside his own feelings? Had he truly been willing to sacrifice his sons for the general welfare of Tinker's Cove?

Maybe the emotional ties between parents and their children grew weaker as the children grew older; after all, Claw's "boys" must be well into their thirties. Lucy rolled back onto her other side and pressed her fanny against Bill spoon-style. Somehow, she didn't think so. She thought of the Whitneys, devastated by the loss of their grown child. She thought of herself, determined to send Toby off to college where he would do what? Get drunk? Try drugs?

Lucy rolled over and rearranged the pillow. Toby didn't have to go to college to try drugs; drugs were readily available in Tinker's Cove. Barney knew it, Ted knew it. What had he said? That he was grateful he hadn't had to report any arrests in Tinker's Cove?

Why not, wondered Lucy. There were plenty of arrests in neighboring towns; the court report in the Portland daily was full of them. Why weren't drug offenders and dealers getting arrested in Tinker's Cove? Lucy thought of the fire, the heroism out front, and the thievery that was going on behind the scenes. She thought of Main Street, the picture-perfect New England town where people didn't bother to lock their doors but where high-school kids were getting illegal drugs.

And she thought of Tucker, supposedly killed by a jealous lover. Except the lover hadn't been all that jealous, from what she'd heard. And Tucker hadn't really seemed like the sort of girl to encourage attention from a married man twice her age.

Lucy flopped onto her back and stared at the ceiling, gray in the dim light from the hall nightlight. Above its smooth blankness, she knew, was a jumble of wires and insulation, a century's worth of dust, insect colonies and, no doubt, families of mice. Tinker's Cove was the same, she thought, a quaint little fishing town with a drug problem.

Under the covers, Lucy shivered and stared at the clock. It was almost two. She had to be up at six, and she had a long day ahead of her. She was going to get to the bottom of this; she was going to find out what was really going on, and a good place to start would be to take another look at Tucker's murder. She snuggled down deeper under the covers and pressed her body against Bill's. She closed her eyes and matched her breathing to his. She slept.

Next thing she knew it was morning. She woke feeling tired and a look in the mirror wasn't reassuring; her eyes were puffy, and she suspected it was going to be a bad hair day. In the kitchen, Zoe was singing Christmas carols and pouring milk into a bowl already overflowing with Cheerios.

"For Pete's sake, Zoe, watch what you're doing," she grumbled, pouring herself a cup of coffee.

"Who's Pete?" chirped Zoe.

Lucy gave her an evil look.

"Well, I see we have lots of Christmas spirit this morning," said Bill.

"Ho, ho, ho," growled Lucy, hanging on to her coffee mug as if it were a life preserver.

Bill studied her, then sighed. "I'll make the lunches," he said.

"Thanks." Lucy fought the impulse to rest her head on the table and took a swallow of coffee.

After a shower and two more cups of coffee Lucy felt almost human. Ted didn't even look up when she arrived at *The Pennysaver,* just grunted and told her he needed the story on the meeting ASAP.

"And make it short," he said. "Space is going to be tight this week."

Lucy took him at his word and tapped out six inches of copy, reporting the results of the vote and adding a quote or two representing the differing points of view expressed at the meeting. It was still early when she left the office, so she decided to head for the gym. If she hurried she could catch Krissy's ten-thirty workout. Lord knows, she could use it, but what was more to the point, hadn't Sue told her that Tucker took a tai chi class after work?

■ ■ ■ ■

"Hi, Lucy," Krissy greeted her, annoyingly pert in a high-cut orange leotard. "You look as if you've got the holiday blues."

"I'm trying my darnedest to get some holiday spirit, but it's awfully hard this year, with the murder and the fire and all."

Keeping up her spirits never seemed to be a problem for Krissy, who had opened the Body Works a few years ago. Even her ponytail bounced, as if it were full of energy, but her face was solemn as she nodded in agreement.

"I know. I just can't believe that creep killed Tucker. . . ." Her gaze wandered to some other clients who were coming through the door, and she raised her voice a few decibels. "You've come to the right place. We'll warm you up, stretch you out, work those muscles and finish up with a relaxing cooldown. You'll feel like a new person when we're done."

"Can I talk to you after class?" asked Lucy as she handed over her five dollars.

Krissy nodded grimly and Lucy gave her hand a squeeze, then headed for the locker room.

■ ■ ■ ■

When the session was over, Lucy had to admit that although she didn't feel exactly like a new person, she did feel like a much-improved version of the old one as she headed down the carpeted corridor to Krissy's office.

Krissy was on the phone, but she smiled at Lucy and pointed to a chair. "I'm on hold — I'm trying to get airplane tickets. All of a sudden I have this irrational urge to go home for Christmas."

"Good luck," said Lucy.

"Yeah. You're right." Krissy put the receiver back in its cradle. "I'll never get tickets this close to Christmas." She rolled her eyes. "I don't know what I was thinking. My family is completely screwed up. I swore I'd never go through another holiday with them, and here I am, ready to spend top dollar to fly to Jersey City just so they can tell me how worthless I am. I think I'll stay here, and have Christmas with Earl."

Earl was Krissy's black Labrador. Pictures of his progress from puppyhood to maturity were plastered all over her office walls, and Earl himself was sound asleep on a futon in the corner.

"Earl's good company," said Lucy.

"The best," affirmed Krissy. "Don't tell him, but I got him a new collar and a squeaky toy for Christmas. Plus a case of tennis balls."

"Mint-flavored?"

"I thought about it, but I decided he really likes them kind of dirt-flavored, and the mint might interfere with the proper aging process."

Lucy laughed. "So Earl is the man in your life these days?"

"You know it." Krissy shook her head. "Face it. There's not much night life in a town like this, except the video store." She sighed. "I really miss Tucker. We had some good times together." Krissy stared at a point above Lucy's head and blinked furiously.

"I didn't realize you were such good friends," said Lucy.

"Well, you know how it is in a small town like this. There aren't that many young, single women. We met here and we hit it off right away. She was such a sweetheart — why'd he have to do it? What a bastard."

"Maybe Steve didn't do it," said Lucy slowly.

"He did it all right," said Krissy. "You wouldn't believe what an unattached woman goes through in this town."

Lucy looked puzzled.

"Tucker loved to dance, you know? So one night we went out to this bar, Scalliwags, they've got live music there on weekends. It's kind of a dump, but we thought what the hell. So we're having a great time dancing with these guys but they get the wrong idea. They think that dancing with them means you want to bear their children, you know what I mean?"

Lucy knew. "Is that what it was with Steve? That he wanted more than she wanted to give?"

Krissy shrugged.

"He just doesn't seem to me like the kind of guy . . ." began Lucy.

Krissy snorted. "They're all the same, believe me. And they're all available — it's just their wives don't know it."

Lucy chuckled. "Don't want to know, is more like it." She paused. "But I heard that Steve and Lee were getting back together."

"Maybe. That doesn't change the fact he was sniffing around Tucker like Earl used to do to the lady dogs before his trip to the vet."

"Okay. I give up. Steve's a worthless scum, but I still think there's a big difference between acting like a hound dog and killing somebody." She scratched her chin. "You know, an awful lot of drugs have been coming through town lately. . . ."

Krissy made her eyes round, pretending to be shocked. "No way."

Lucy continued. "I was just wondering if Tucker might have got involved somehow, got in too deep or something."

"Whoa." Krissy held up her hands to protest. "Are you kidding? Tucker wouldn't touch drugs with a ten-foot pole. Do you know who her father is?"

Lucy shook her head.

"He's a big shot in the Department of Justice, I mean way up there. Just under the attorney general, I think. Anyway, he's head prosecutor for all the federal drug cases."

"I had no idea."

Krissy nodded. " 'Just say no' is like a religion in that family."

"Yeah, but, look at yourself. Kids don't always agree with their parents."

"Tucker did. Believe me. She used to say she didn't see why people couldn't just get high on life. Nature, the woods, skiing, sailing, she used to come back from those AMC hikes all excited about the trees and the clouds, for Pete's sake."

Lucy wondered if she'd heard right. "AMC hikes?"

"Yeah. You know, Appalachian Mountain Club. Tucker was a member."

So that was what the notation in Tucker's agenda meant, thought Lucy. She hadn't met Lee that Sunday before she'd died, she'd gone for a hike.

"Does anybody else around here belong? Anybody I could talk to?"

"Sure. Witt's actually the president, I think."

"Witt?"

"He teaches kick boxing." Krissy glanced at her watch. "That reminds me. It's time for me to kick butt."

"Kick butt?" asked Lucy, standing up to go.

"That's what I call it. It's a class for women who want to tighten and firm their bottoms. We have it at noon so the working gals can come."

"Oh." She walked down the hall with Krissy. "I hope you and Earl have a merry Christmas."

"We're gonna do our best," said Krissy, as she pulled open the gym door. Lucy peeked through the door, wondering if she knew anybody in the class, and recognized Steffie Scott. She tried to catch her eye, but Steffie was too absorbed in her thoughts to notice her.

Lucy paused in the entryway, studying the bulletin board as she zipped her parka, looking for the class schedule among the clutter of posters and announcements. There, under a notice advertising an amateur performance of *The Nutcracker* she saw a bright yellow sheet of paper announcing AMC hikes every Sunday at one o'clock. Next to it was the schedule: Witt's kickboxing class was at three-thirty on weekday afternoons.

Swinging her gym bag over her shoulder, Lucy headed for the car. She'd get some lunch and do some last-minute shopping, she decided, and then she'd try to catch Witt before his class.

CHAPTER EIGHTEEN

The backseat of Lucy's car was filled with bags of goodies and stocking stuffers when she returned to the Body Works at twenty past three. She hesitated for a moment in the vestibule, wondering how to approach Witt, when she saw a young man in exercise clothes coming out of the office with a sheet of paper in his hand. He stopped at the reception desk and started to poke around in a drawer, obviously looking for something.

Lucy walked over to the desk and he looked up. "Can I help you?" he asked.

"I'm looking for Witt."

"That's me," he said, with a lopsided smile.

Lucy smiled back. Witt had the easy manner of someone who was comfortable with himself and knew he could handle pretty much any problem that came up. He wasn't very tall and at first glance seemed rather stocky, but he was all muscle.

"I'm interested in these AMC hikes," she began. "Can you tell me anything about them?"

"Sure," he said, opening an Altoids tin and plucking a thumbtack out of the assortment of paper clips and other small, useful items it contained. He held up the paper for her to see and walked over to the bulletin board, bouncing on the balls of his feet as he went.

"See, this is the schedule. We have a different hike every Sunday." He rearranged the papers on the bulletin board and made a space for his new notice, then turned to Lucy. "There's no charge or anything, but we kind of encourage people to become AMC members if they become regulars."

"That's fair enough," said Lucy, noticing that his eyes were very blue indeed. "I think a friend of mine was a member — Tucker Whitney?"

"Yeah." He looked down, studying his hands. He swallowed and Lucy saw his Adam's apple bob, a little bulge in the middle of his size 18 neck. "That was too bad."

"Did you know her well?"

"Just from the hikes. She almost always came." He seemed to be choosing his words carefully. "It's not going to be the same without her."

"I know." Lucy's voice was gentle. "I wish I'd had time to get to know her better."

He sighed. "I know what you mean."

Something in his tone made Lucy wonder if he'd had hopes of a serious relationship with Tucker.

"So, what do you do on these hikes?"

"Hike, you know. Follow a trail. Some people take photographs or look for birds." He looked over her shoulder and smiled at one of his students. "Go on in — I'll be with you in a minute."

Lucy felt she was running out of time. "How many people go?"

"Sometimes just two or three, if the weather's really nice we might get eight or nine."

"And that Sunday before she died?"

"Five or six, I think." He nodded at a pair of students who were signing in at the desk. "Tucker was late that day. We waited a good forty-five minutes for her. Usually we wouldn't do that, but nobody wanted to start without her."

Lucy lowered her voice. "Did she seem the same as usual? I mean, could she have been stoned or something?"

"Tucker?" His voice was sharp, and those blue eyes seemed to bore right through her.

Lucy felt she had to defend her question. "I heard some things."

"About Tucker?" His tone implied she couldn't have been more wrong.

Lucy shrugged.

"That's ridiculous. Who told you that?" He looked as if he'd like to smash a fist into whoever had suggested Tucker might have used drugs.

"Maybe I got it wrong," said Lucy.

"You sure did. Look, I've got to go. The hike's at one, if you want to come."

"Thanks." Lucy started to go, then turned around and called after him. "Did she say why she was late?"

Witt whirled to face her; the movement was quick, and he was perfectly balanced. "She said she took a wrong turn." Then he vanished into the gym.

Lucy checked the bulletin board for the old schedule, and found it under a notice advertising a slightly used set of barbells. According to the schedule, that Sunday the group had hiked in the conservation area near Smith Heights Road.

That was funny, thought Lucy, as she headed back to her car. Tucker had summered on Smith Heights Road for her entire life — how could she make a wrong turn that would delay her for forty-five minutes?

As she started the car, she considered taking a quick spin out along Smith Heights Road to the conservation area, to see where Tucker might have made her wrong turn. A look at the dashboard clock told her she didn't have time, today. She had a family waiting and a Christmas tree to trim.

The Stones always set up their tree on the last day of school before Christmas vacation, usually the day before Christmas Eve. Nobody quite knew how or why the custom began, but through the years it had taken on the weight of tradition. Now, it was absolutely unthinkable to put up the tree on any other day.

When Lucy arrived home, Bill and Toby had already brought the tree in and set it in its stand and Toby was perched on a stepladder, arranging the strings of lights. Bill was carrying in the boxes of ornaments, Sara was busy digging out the Christmas CDs, and Zoe was a small ball of excitement.

"Hurry, Mom. It's time to trim the tree."

"So I see. But we can't start hanging the ornaments until Toby finishes putting on the lights."

"He's almost done," insisted Zoe, ignoring the coils of wire and bulbs covering the family-room floor.

"Why don't you help Sara find the music?"

"Okay, Mom."

Having distracted Zoe for a moment, Lucy hurried upstairs to hide the bags of stocking stuffers she had bought earlier. That done, she stood outside the room Elizabeth shared with Sara and knocked on the door. The frantic drumbeats of alternative rock told her Elizabeth was inside.

"What?" Elizabeth called out in answer to Lucy's knock.

"We're trimming the tree. Don't you want to help?"

"Do I have to?"

"Don't you want to?"

There was a long silence. "Not really."

Lucy poked the door open and peeked in.

"Is everything OK?" asked Lucy. "Are they giving you a hard time at school?"

"Nah. School's cool." Elizabeth was standing in front of her mirror, considering her appearance.

From the pile of clothes on the bed, Lucy guessed she was trying on outfits. Personally, she didn't think the black fishnet stockings really went with the silky, pink sheath, and the chartreuse sweater was really a mistake.

"Whaddya think?" Elizabeth turned, cock-

259

ing her hip.

"What's the occasion?" asked Lucy.

"Nothing, really." Elizabeth ran her hands through her hair, making it stand up in short spikes.

"You look fine," said Lucy, starting down the stairs. Under her breath she added, "Just don't think you're leaving the house looking like that."

Elizabeth called after her. "Did you say something, Mom?"

"Nothing."

In the kitchen, Lucy found Sara filling a plate with cookies from the cookie jar.

"Good idea. I think I'll make some cocoa, while we wait to get started." Lucy got out a pot. "Is something bothering Elizabeth?"

"Woomph," said Sara, her mouth full of cookie.

"Would you mind repeating that?" Lucy measured cocoa and sugar and dumped them into the pot, then added a quart of milk.

"Lance."

Lance and Elizabeth had been close friends, but this fall Lance had gone away to a private boarding school.

"What about Lance?"

"Susie MacIntyre told Elizabeth that he's home for Christmas, but he hasn't called her yet."

"Oh."

Lucy set the pot on the stove and turned the burner on. She got a spoon out of a drawer and began stirring the mixture, so it wouldn't stick to the bottom. When it was ready she poured the hot chocolate into mugs, set them on a tray and carried it into the family room.

Zoe, she saw as she entered, hadn't been able to resist opening the boxes of ornaments. She'd already unwrapped some of her favorites and had lined them up on the coffee table.

Lucy set the tray down beside them and picked one up. It was a little baby, sleeping in a crescent moon.

"That's Elizabeth's," she told Zoe. "From her first Christmas."

"It's beautiful."

"Yes, it is." Lucy sat down on the couch and took a bite of cookie. She wanted Elizabeth to hang the ornament on the tree, just as she had every year until now. "Why don't you see if she'll come down and hang her ornament?" she suggested.

Happy to have an important errand, Zoe ran off.

"Cookies and cocoa," announced Lucy, noticing that Sara was making quite a dent in the cookies. "Better come and get some before it's all gone."

"I think I'll get a beer," said Bill, heading for the kitchen.

"In a minute," said Toby, reaching for the last string of lights.

Sara had already polished off her mug of cocoa when Zoe returned.

"She said to save it for her. She'll be down in a while."

"Where's Elizabeth?" asked Bill, sitting beside her and tilting back his bottle of beer.

"Sulking in her room."

Lucy watched as Zoe carefully lifted the mug of hot liquid to her lips and took a swallow. "Mmmm," she said, and licked her upper lip with her tongue.

Just then a blast of organ music came from the stereo and a famous choir began singing "Venite Adoramus." Tears sprang to Lucy's eyes as she was overwhelmed with a flood of jumbled emotions from all the Christmases past and for a brief moment she wanted to be a little girl once again, standing in the candlelit, pine-scented church, holding tight to her father's hand.

"Well, let's get started," she said, opening one of the boxes of ornaments and lifting out a bright red ball. She carried it over to the tree and placed it on a branch.

Soon the floor was covered with tissue and newspaper wrappings, and the tree was filling up with decorations. Ordinary glass balls, special ornaments collected on family vacations, pinecones and seashells the children had gathered and coated with glitter when they were little, and a small but precious collection of antique German glass ornaments that had somehow survived scores of clumsy fingers and hundreds of Christmases.

Lucy was watching as Zoe hung one of the very oldest, a glass fish so old that the paint had become translucent, when the phone rang. Zoe immediately lost interest in the ornament and turned toward the phone, ready to race Sara and Toby to answer it. Lucy quickly snatched the ornament from her, letting out a sigh of relief as she twisted the bit of wire that served as a hook securely onto a high branch.

This time, Sara won the dash for the phone. "Elizabeth!" she shrieked. "It's Lance!"

Disappointed the call wasn't for them, the other children turned back to trimming the tree. In a few minutes, Elizabeth joined them. Ignoring everyone's curious glances, she picked her ornament off the coffee table and hung it on a branch.

"Is it OK if I go out for a while?" she asked, casually.

"Lance asked her out!" Zoe was fascinated by the whole idea of romance and dating.

"Is that true?" asked Lucy. "What are your plans?"

"Just to hang out," Elizabeth murmured, nervously twisting a strand of hair.

"That's unacceptable," said Bill, decisively placing a candy cane on the end of a branch.

"What do you mean?" demanded Elizabeth.

"Well, this is a family night," began Lucy.

"You mean I can't go?"

Lucy looked to Bill for support.

"I don't mind if you go out," he said. "You haven't exactly added a lot to the occasion so far. But I don't want you hanging out in some car at the end of a dark lane. And you certainly can't go looking like that. Put some slacks on."

"Dad!" Elizabeth was indignant.

"Well, I don't think you should go out at all," insisted Lucy. "Why not invite Lance to join us here, decorating the tree?"

"Oh, Mom," groaned Elizabeth, then ran out of the room. They could all hear her thumping up the stairs in her platform shoes.

"That went well," said Bill, facetiously, as

he reached up and set the star on the top of the tree.

"She'll sulk in her room all night," said Lucy.

"Not a problem for me," said Bill, pleased to have thwarted one of his daughter's suitors. "How about I call for some pizza?"

"Great idea." Lucy wrapped her arms around his waist and hugged him.

Elizabeth declined to join the rest of the family for their pizza supper, but that didn't stop the other kids from enjoying their treat. When every scrap of pizza was gone, and the room had been cleared of papers and ornament boxes, Bill switched on the tree and turned off the lamps. They all stood for a moment, admiring the lighted, decorated tree.

"It's magic," sighed Zoe.

"It's the best one ever," said Sara.

"Neat," said Toby.

Later, while everyone was watching Christmas videos on TV, Lucy slipped upstairs to talk to Elizabeth. She found her sprawled on her bed amidst most of her clothes, talking on the phone. On the bookcase, her little pink TV was playing.

Lucy stood, not knowing where to start. Why couldn't she take better care of her clothes, instead of leaving them draped all over? Why was she always, always on the phone? And why was the TV on, when she obviously wasn't watching it?

Lucy reached out, to switch it off, but was caught momentarily by the drama. It was an old black-and-white gangster movie, with actors she didn't recognize.

"He's gettin' to be a problem," growled one gangster, talking around a huge cigar.

"What do you want?" Elizabeth was glaring at her from the bed.

Lucy wanted to sit beside her, to hug her, but there was no place to sit. "I just wanted you to know that Daddy and I only want what's best for you."

"Yeah? Well, why won't you trust me? All I wanted to do was spend some time with my friends," demanded Elizabeth.

"He's not goin' along with the program," commented another gangster, a small fellow with a wizened face.

"That's why," said Lucy, pointing to the TV. "I trust you to do what's right, but I don't trust all your friends."

"I can take care of myself," insisted Elizabeth.

"He knows too much. We gotta rub him out." It was the gangster with the cigar.

Stunned, Lucy sat down on the bed, staring at the TV.

Elizabeth reached out and turned it off, and the picture shrank to a little, bright dot.

Suddenly, Lucy knew why Tucker had been killed. She had been a good girl, a girl her parents trusted not to get into trouble. And she hadn't done anything wrong herself, but she had seen something she shouldn't have, probably during that forty-five minutes she was supposedly lost before the hike. She had known too much. And that made her dangerous to somebody. Her innocence hadn't protected her; it had made her vulnerable.

"Mom, are you OK?"

Lucy nodded, and pulled Elizabeth close to her.

CHAPTER NINETEEN

1 day 'til Xmas

Lucy had just slipped the chocolate cheese-cake into the oven and was starting to make lunch for herself and the girls, Toby having been recruited to act as Bill's gofer, when she realized she was ready for Christmas. The long month's preparations were done. The cards and packages had been sent, the presents had been bought and wrapped, the house decorated and the tree trimmed, the refrigerator and pantry were stocked with holiday treats.

"Do you girls have any plans for this afternoon?" she asked, as they gathered around the kitchen table to eat tuna fish sandwiches and tomato soup. "Zoe, you've been invited to go to Sadie's house to make gingerbread men."

"Cool," said Zoe, prompting Lucy to raise an eyebrow. They sure grew up fast these days.

"I'm supposed to go ice-skating with Jenn," said Sara. "Mrs. Baker said she'd pick me up at one."

"That sounds like fun. What about you, Elizabeth?"

"Lance wants me to go over to his house to go swimming."

"Isn't it kind of cold for swimming?" Lucy took a bite of sandwich.

"They got an indoor pool."

Lucy choked on a bit of tuna fish that went down the wrong way. "An indoor pool?"

She knew Lance's mother, Norah Hemmings, better known as the "queen of daytime TV," was a wealthy woman, but this was definitely a first for Tinker's Cove.

"Yeah. He's invited a bunch of us to come over and hang out. I can go, can't I, Mom?"

"Only if you bring back a complete report," specified Lucy. "Sue will want to know all the details."

"Deal."

It was one-thirty when Lucy pulled into Norah Hemmings's driveway, after dropping Zoe at the Orensteins'. True enough, she saw that a large addition with huge French windows had been added to the back of the big mansion on Smith Heights

269

Road. Norah's house now dwarfed the neighboring houses, including Corney and Chuck Canaday's, which stood next door.

"Dad's going to pick you up on his way home, around four."

"Why don't I just call, instead," suggested Elizabeth.

"No way, Jose," said Lucy, firmly nipping that idea in the bud. "And listen. If I hear the slightest rumor that anything went on here that shouldn't have, you can count on being grounded for the rest of vacation. Understand?"

"Oh, Mom," groaned Elizabeth, as she climbed out of the car. "You can trust me."

"Right," muttered Lucy to herself, as she turned the car around in the spacious driveway.

As Lucy drove past one impressive house after another, all with spectacular ocean views, she couldn't help wondering why anybody would want to live here year-round. A bone-chilling wind came right off the ocean, she could feel it pushing against the Subaru. And the ocean wasn't much to look at on a gray day when you couldn't tell where water ended and sky began. In the distant sky she could see two herring gulls. One, an immature brown one had a fish, she could see silvery flashes as it struggled to break free. The other, a mature white-and-gray bird, was darting at the younger bird, trying to make him drop his prize. The brownish gull held on stubbornly, but the fish finally wriggled free and fell through the air, only to be scooped up by the more experienced bird, who flapped off in triumph. The yearling gull complained against this injustice. His harsh, hollow call echoed in Lucy's ears as she passed a mailbox marked WHITNEY.

Acting on impulse, Lucy braked and stopped the car. She looked at the house, a big old wooden box ringed by a generous porch, no doubt filled with chintz-cushioned wicker chairs in the summer but now bare and empty. Long window boxes had been filled with geraniums, now black stumps shriveled by frost. Lucy shuddered, thinking of Tucker all alone in that big, hollow house.

She drove on down the road, surprised to come upon the conservation area only a quarter mile or so from the Whitney house. Once again, Lucy thought it unlikely that Tucker had lost her way, as she had told her fellow hikers. She had summered in that house for her whole life; she must have known about the conservation area.

Saying she was lost must have been an excuse. Something must have delayed her, and it must have been something she didn't want to talk about. Something she felt she had to cover up. What could it be?

Lucy looked up at the Whitney house, and realized it was built on an outcropping of rock that set it up higher than the neighboring houses. In fact, it was so high that someone standing in one of the upstairs windows would have a clear view out to sea, looking right over the roofs of the houses on the other side of the road. From there, Lucy realized, Tucker could see the boats coming and going from Tinker's Cove, and with a pair of binoculars she could probably see the big freighters farther out at sea on their way to Halifax.

What if Tucker had seen something out of the ordinary, as she looked out of those big windows, thought Lucy. What if whatever it was she saw made her so curious that she went to investigate? Reaching to the end of Smith Heights Road, Lucy was about to turn out onto the main road when she noticed a well-worn dirt road branching down toward the water. Impulsively, she decided to see where it led. After all, she had no other responsibilities this afternoon. It was hers to spend as she liked.

The Subaru bounced along, rocking from side to side and crunching through icy patches, for a few hundred feet. Then the road opened out and Lucy found herself looking at a cluster of metal buildings. A small sign read ROUSSEAU'S LOBSTERS.

Nobody seemed to be around, there were no cars or trucks, so Lucy turned off the ignition and got out of the car. A blast of cold wind blowing off the water hit her, and she shivered, pulling up the hood of her parka and stuffing her hands in the pockets as she began walking across the yard to the dock. This wasn't at all what she expected a lobster pound to be; she had somehow imagined the lobsters would be kept in some sort of pen or corral in the water. But there was nothing like that, only a dock with a hoist at the end, for unloading the boats. The holding pens must be in the metal buildings, she decided, so the workers could stay relatively warm and dry. Reaching the end of the dock she stood a minute, scanning the empty cove. The wind rattled the line on the hoist; it creaked as it swung back and forth. Realizing her teeth were chattering, she turned to go back to the car and saw she had company. A pickup truck was now parked next to her car, and two men were coming towards her.

Recognizing Rusty and J.J., Lucy gave a

wave and a big smile, but they didn't smile back.

"What are you doing here?" demanded J.J., when they were within earshot.

"I was looking for lobsters," improvised Lucy. "For Christmas dinner."

Rusty and J.J. exchanged uneasy glances.

"Isn't that what the sign says? Lobsters?" asked Lucy, cocking her head.

The two men were standing opposite her, blocking her path to the car, a situation Lucy wasn't entirely comfortable with. In fact, she would have been a lot happier in her car, speeding back home. Snooping around suddenly didn't seem like such a good idea.

J.J. shook his head, and a lock of curly dark hair fell across his forehead. "We only do wholesale," he said.

"Yeah," agreed Rusty, scratching the orange stubble on his chin. "And with the quota and all, we don't have any extras."

Lucy shrugged her shoulders. "Well, that's too bad. I guess I'll have to try someplace else."

Much to her relief the two men courteously stepped aside, clearing the path to her car.

"Merry Christmas," she said, reaching for the door handle, when she heard the sound of a boat motor. They all looked up as a boat approached the dock, then turned abruptly as a red pickup truck sped into the yard and stopped suddenly, brakes squealing. The driver-side door flew open and Claw jumped down and ran toward them.

"What's going on?" he demanded, pointing a stubby finger at Lucy. "What's she doing here?"

"She wants lobsters," J.J. explained. "I told her we only sell wholesale."

"Don't you know who she is?" Claw was looking past them, out to the dock. "She's that newspaper reporter. From the meeting the other night."

Rusty looked over his shoulder to the dock, where a man was tying up the boat. "Is that true?"

"I write for the paper," began Lucy, as Claw began running to the boat, waving his arms. "Mostly features, you know, soft stuff. In fact," she extemporized, checking her watch. "I'm supposed to interview Mrs. Santa Claus — to get the behind-the-scenes story — and I'm a little late. So, Merry Christmas to you and your families."

Determined not to look back no matter what happened she grabbed the handle and pulled the car door open. Stepping next to her, Rusty slammed it shut.

"I think the old man wants to talk to you," he said, roughly grabbing her arm. Before she could protest, J.J. had her other arm and they were dragging her toward one of the buildings. A door was opened, and she was roughly thrust inside. "You wait here," he said, and the door slammed shut.

"You can't do this to me," she screamed. Nobody answered. The door remained shut. Lucy looked around. She was in a dim, chilly room with a concrete floor. Light came through translucent plastic panels on the roof, and she could make out big vats lined up in rows. She peered in the nearest one and saw a few dozen lobsters resting on the bottom.

She stood there, looking at them, wondering how she could have been so stupid. She had retraced Tucker's steps all too well; only to be trapped herself. Whatever Tucker had found had gotten her killed. Lucy was determined that wasn't going to happen to her. She began exploring the room, looking for a way to escape.

It only took minutes to discover that there were no windows and only the one door. She turned the knob, but it was locked. She looked up at the roof, wondering how solid the light panels were, when she heard voices approaching. When a few minutes had passed, and the door didn't open, she pressed her ear against the crack, hoping to hear what they were saying.

"I don't like this business. We should never've locked her up. Now what are we gonna do with her? Say, gee, sorry about that, don't tell anybody, and we'll let you go. *Joyeux Noël* and all that?"

Sounds good to me, Lucy thought hopefully.

"What else could we do?" It sounded like J.J. "The stuff's coming in and we've got a newspaper reporter right here. . . ."

Lucy's breath caught. She could hardly believe what she had heard. They really were dealing in illegal drugs.

"Let me tell you," continued J.J. "There's something wrong with this picture, and what's wrong is that broad being here."

Lucy felt her cheeks redden.

"No, what's wrong with this picture is that we ever got involved in the first place." That was Rusty, Lucy thought, straining to hear every word. "We're in so deep, how're we ever gonna get out?"

Lucy saw a dim ray of hope. Maybe she could convince them that tossing her in with the lobsters or whatever they planned to do with her would only make things worse. She heard the rattle of keys and stepped back from the door just in time.

It opened, and Claw entered, followed by his two sons.

"What's your name?" he asked.

"Lucy Stone. I live in town with my husband and four children. They're probably wondering what's keeping me."

Claw nodded. "You tell me, what exactly brought you out here?"

"Lobsters — for Christmas." Lucy decided to stick with her story. "Do you treat all your customers like this? Lock them up?"

Behind Claw, J.J. was smiling. "Sorry about that. It's just that, well, you heard about this quota?"

"Yeah, that's it," said Rusty. "We've got too many lobsters. We're way above quota. And you're not gonna tell anybody about it, because I'm gonna give you some of these lobsters. That makes you guilty, too, right?"

"Right." Lucy watched as J.J. picked up a wooden stick with a hook on the end and went over to the tank. He began pulling out lobsters and putting them in a burlap sack, and she felt a huge sense of relief. She was actually going to get out of here.

"How many you want?" he asked.

"Just one," she said. "Like a dollar to seal a contract."

"Nah," said Claw. "You said four kids.

Give her six, six nice ones. For Christmas dinner."

"Thank you so much." Lucy took the sack. "Believe me, I won't say a word about this to anyone."

"Not even Mrs. Santa Claus?" Claw's eyes gleamed mischievously.

"Not even her."

Claw opened the door for her. "Rusty, those are heavy. You carry them for the lady."

"I can manage," protested Lucy, to no avail. Rusty insisted on escorting her to her car. He opened the door for her, and carefully placed the sack of lobsters in the back.

"Safe home," he said, before he slammed the hatchback down.

Her hands were shaking so badly Lucy could hardly get the key in the ignition. When it finally slipped in and turned, and the car started, she felt tears streaming down her face. It was as if she had been given a wonderful gift, a gift she didn't deserve, and she felt humble and thankful and guilty and incredibly lucky all at once. She shifted into gear and lifted her foot off the brake, and began slowly turning the car around toward the driveway. She pressed her foot on the gas, accelerating toward the drive, when a police cruiser suddenly appeared, blocking the way out and leaving her with no choice but to slam on the brakes.

Chapter Twenty

When Tom Scott emerged from the police cruiser Lucy had mixed emotions. She didn't really want the Rousseaus to get in trouble, but she couldn't condone drug dealing, and that was what she suspected they were up to.

She gave Tom a big smile and a wave, expecting him to move his car when he saw who she was, but that didn't happen. He only gave her a glance and went straight over to Rusty and J.J. Lucy figured the best course of action was to stay in her car, continuing the pretense that she was only there to pick up some lobsters.

She didn't even turn her head to observe their discussion; she wanted to make it clear she was minding her own business, but she could see them in the rearview mirror. Scott was clearly the one in charge. She could tell from J.J.'s and Rusty's bowed heads and restrained gestures that they were not challenging him, but that was to be expected. Nobody argued with a cop, not even at a traffic stop, unless they wanted to get into more trouble. So she sat and waited for Scott to move the cruiser.

The men finally appeared to finish their discussion and Lucy watched as Tom walked across the yard toward the two cars, expecting him to finally move the cruiser and wave her on. Instead, he stopped next to her and yanked the door open.

"Out," he said.

"What's this all about?" she asked, unfastening her seat belt. "I'd really like to get home with my lobsters."

"You're not going anywhere," he said, roughly turning her around and shoving her against the car. "Hands behind your back."

Lucy had seen enough movies to know what that meant — she was about to be handcuffed. She turned her head, and started to protest.

"I said, hands behind your back," growled Scott.

Reluctantly, she obeyed and discovered that being handcuffed was a lot more uncomfortable than it looked, especially if you were wearing a bulky parka. The next step, she supposed, was to be placed in "the cage" in the back of his cruiser. But instead,

Tom pulled her in the other direction, toward the lobster pound office, where she was thrown into a hard, wooden chair. Her upper arm, which had taken the brunt of the impact, felt sore and bruised.

"Don't move," he warned her.

Confused and frightened, Lucy nodded.

He opened the door to leave, but stepped back as an enraged Claw Rousseau came charging in.

"What do you think you're doing?" Claw bellowed at him. "This is my place! You got no business here!"

Scott grinned at him. It wasn't a very nice grin, thought Lucy, trying to make herself as small and inconspicuous as she could.

"You know how it works. You're behind." Scott shook his head. "The retirement fund's not growing the way it's supposed to. You missed last month, you haven't paid anything yet this month. What's going on? I thought we had a deal."

"We've got a deal," said Claw, looking nervously past Scott to Lucy. "You'll get it, don't worry. But you've got to let her go. She doesn't know anything about this."

Scott glanced at Lucy, and she cringed in the chair. "You know who she is? She's a reporter. She's been snooping all over town."

Claw raised his hands to protest, but Scott cut him off.

"Look, right now, she's my problem. I'll take care of her."

Lucy swallowed hard. That didn't sound good. She strained to hear as Scott lowered his voice and led Claw across the room, toward the door.

"You've got problems of your own. I just picked up some interesting information on the radio — a couple of your associates from Boston have been spotted on the turnpike. They might be headed here, you think?"

The door flew open again and Lucy jumped in spite of herself. The thumping in her chest slowed when she realized it was only Rusty and J.J.

"Did you hear?" Claw's tone was urgent. "The guys from Boston are coming here."

Rusty looked stricken, as if he'd been punched in the heart.

"They want Russ Junior," he said.

J.J. wrapped an arm around his smaller brother's shoulder.

"We'll take care of 'Ti-Russ," he said. "We'll put him on the boat, send him up the coast. These guys are city boys. They won't find him."

Lucy struggled to follow their conversation. 'Ti-Russ, she knew, was short for Petit

Russ, Rusty's son. She remembered him as a sturdy little fellow on Toby's youth soccer team. He'd be in high school now, she thought.

"That's no good." Rusty's eyes were wide. "They don't find Russ, they'll kill us, or our wives and kids. Burn down the house — they don't care. They just want to send a message." He buried his head in his hands. "I can't believe he was so stupid, what he got us into."

"He's a kid. Kids are stupid." Claw shrugged. "We'll get the money; they'll go away."

Lucy remembered Toby and Eddie refusing to tell her who was dealing drugs in the high school. Now she had a pretty good idea that it was 'Ti-Russ. What had he done? Helped himself to part of a shipment, shorting the buyer and putting his whole family in peril?

"So where are we gonna get the money?" demanded Rusty, his voice breaking.

"Take it easy," said Scott. "It's under control. The drug task force is on to them — it's just a matter of time before those guys are out of the picture. You lie low, keep your young entrepreneur under wraps for a while. Go on, get started. Get on out of here." He glanced at Lucy. "I'll take care of

Miss Snoopy."

The three men seemed to confer silently for a moment, then Claw nodded, and they shuffled out of the room. Not one of them looked at her.

Left alone with Scott, Lucy's situation hit her with a thudding certainty. She knew way too much. Scott was going to kill her, just as he'd killed Tucker.

CHAPTER
TWENTY-ONE

Not if she could help it, she vowed to herself. She was going to get out of this. Nobody, especially a mealy-mouthed hypocrite like Tom Scott, was going to wreck her family's Christmas. She glanced around frantically, looking for something, anything. The drug task force was supposed to be in the area. If only she could draw their attention somehow, anybody's attention, maybe she could save herself. She needed time, and the only way she could think of getting it was by keeping him talking.

"You sure had me fooled," said Lucy. "I never would have picked you for Tucker's murderer."

She was surprised to find her voice strong and steady. At that moment she wasn't afraid of Tom Scott; she was disgusted by him. He had come into town under the banner of zero tolerance for drugs and alcohol, and he even had his wife passing out Mothers Against Drunk Driving pamphlets. While he was mouthing sticky sentiments about the tragedy of teen drunken driving deaths he was turning a blind eye on the drugs that were pouring into town and collecting kickbacks. Retirement fund. She snorted.

"I wouldn't be so cocky if I were you," he said. "Tucker Whitney was a stupid bitch who got herself caught in the wrong place at the wrong time, same as you. Came snooping around here and the Rousseaus scared her off, so you know what she did? Actually called me up to report suspicious activity."

He gave a short, harsh laugh and stepped toward her. Lucy felt her courage disappear like dirty dishwater swirling down the drain. She was utterly defenseless, hands pinned behind her back. She wanted to run, but she couldn't make her legs work. Horrified, she watched as he took another step closer.

How many seconds did she have to live? Was he really going to put his hands around her neck and strangle her, like he did Tucker? She couldn't let that happen.

"I have to hand it to you," she said, struggling to make the words come out of her dry mouth. "You're pretty clever. You planted that gum wrapper, didn't you?"

"It was so easy," Scott said, unable to

resist telling her how he'd outsmarted everybody. "I knew I had to get rid of Tucker — she was starting to make a real pest of herself, calling the station and asking what I was going to do about the lobster pound. She even threatened to call the drug task force. Then I ran into Cummings at the coffee shop. He'd just left Tucker and he was real broken up. He couldn't wait to tell me all about it. How he was going to give her up and go back to his wife, even if it was the hardest thing he'd ever done. She'd been understanding, he said, actually encouraged him to do the right thing."

"From what I heard she didn't really care for him," said Lucy, hoping to keep Scott's mind off the next item on his agenda. It was all she could think to do. Every second she could delay his assault was a small victory. Maybe the Rousseaus would come back. Maybe help would come.

"Yeah, I heard that, too. But to hear him it was the love affair of the century. He was practically crying into his coffee, and popping those sticks of gum into his mouth one after the other. He finished the pack and left it on the counter. I figured it might come in handy and picked it up with a napkin." He grinned evilly. "I was right. I called her up from a pay phone and asked if

I could come over to her house to get a statement from her before she went to work. She was only too happy to cooperate."

"You even won a commendation from the state police for preventing contamination of the crime scene. That must have been icing on the cake."

"It just goes to show that if you do a really good job, people notice," said Scott, practically patting himself on the back. "But you know what the best part was? It was the look in Tucker's eyes when she realized that Officer Scott wasn't her friend."

He was now standing above her, and Lucy felt his leather-gloved hands closing around her neck. She squirmed, trying to kick between his legs, but he just laughed and pressed her legs down with his. She tried to scream, but nothing was coming out, she couldn't make a sound, she couldn't catch her breath. Then it came, a popping sound, and everything went dark in the room.

"What the fuck," she heard him say, and he dropped his hands from her neck. She assumed he was moving toward the window, so she ran in the opposite direction, knocking something over as she dashed across the room and crashed into the big wooden desk. She felt her way around it, putting it between herself and Scott.

She heard the door open and for a second saw Scott's figure silhouetted against the dim dusky light outside, and then he disappeared.

Her heart was pounding. This was her chance to escape and she had to take it. She ran to the door and cautiously opened it, intending to take a cautious peek to see if the coast was clear. Instead, she was suddenly blinded by an extremely bright light that was flooding the yard. She heard popping gunshots and ducked back inside.

What with the spotlights and guns, it seemed to her that the entire compound was under attack. She got down as low as she could and scuttled awkwardly across the floor, diving under the desk. She landed hard on her shoulder; she couldn't use her handcuffed hands to break the fall.

There was the piercing squeal of an amplifier and then an authoritarian voice boomed out. "This is the state police. Drop your weapons. Put your hands on your heads. Walk to the lighted area."

Thank God, thought Lucy, who was only too happy to obey. She couldn't put her hands on her head, but she could walk. She crawled out from under the desk, blinking her eyes against the light that was pouring in through the windows, and started toward the doorway, only to be immediately knocked off her feet. Scott had come back.

"Get up," he said, yanking her to her feet and holding her in front of him like a shield. "You're my ticket out of here."

The pain in her shoulder was agonizing as she struggled against his grip.

"Let her go." Lucy recognized J.J.'s voice. She heard a thud and felt Scott's body crumple behind her. "I've wanted to do that for a long time," he said.

Lucy found herself in wholehearted agreement. "Me too," she heard herself say. "Get me out of these handcuffs?"

J.J. began going through Scott's pockets, feeling for his keys while Lucy kept an eye on the door. It was quiet outside; the gunshots had stopped.

"Got 'em!" exclaimed J.J. "Hold still," he said, grasping her arm.

She bit her lip, refusing to cry out with the pain. First one cuff and then the other loosened, and she moaned with relief. She cradled her arm against her chest, watching as J.J. clamped one cuff on Scott's wrist and then, with a grunt, dragged his inert body to the corner, where he looped the other cuff around the gas pipe that fed the overhead heater.

"That takes care of Dudley Doright," he

said, with a satisfied smirk. "Now, the heroic Jean-Jacques, having saved the lady in distress, gives himself up to the authorities. Ready?"

"You bet," said Lucy.

J.J. took her hand and reached for the door, but before they could step out into the light they heard the staccato of machine-gun fire, and it suddenly went dark again.

"What's going on?" Lucy gripped his hand tighter as they ducked back into the shelter of the office.

"Fatman." J.J.'s voice was a moan. "He loves that Uzi. I never saw him without it."

"It couldn't be," whispered Lucy. "Nobody'd take on an entire SWAT team."

"Nobody but Fatman. They named him after the atom bomb. I heard nothing can stop him. He shot five or six cops last time they tried."

"What about Rusty and Claw? Where are they?"

"On the boat. They're gone."

Lucy was stunned. "You could've gone — why didn't you?"

She felt his breath on her cheek as he sighed.

"I had enough. You know how all this started? We took out the boat and picked up one little package and brought it in.

Never saw nobody. Just left it on top of a trash can in a highway rest area. That was gonna be it. Pay the bills, get a fresh start. But it don't work that way. Scott shows up. Somehow he knows all about it. He wants a cut, or he'll turn us in. 'Ti-Russ gets ahold of some, he starts dealing, and then he starts using and he's high all the time. Pretty soon we've got more dope than lobsters goin' through here, and the weird thing is, we're not gettin' any richer. What's worse, we're scared all the time. Scared of the cops. Scared of Fatman and his friends." He inched up the wall and looked out the window. "I wish I knew what was going on out there."

"Me too." Lucy found herself giggling.

"What's so funny?"

"I was just thinking about my family. They're probably wondering where I am and why there's no supper. They probably think I went Christmas shopping and forgot the time, or something like that. They'd never believe where I really am."

"I don't believe it, and I'm here." J.J. slumped against the wall beneath the window, next to her.

Across the room, she heard Scott stirring.

"He'll get us all killed," muttered J.J., standing up.

He hadn't taken a step when his body was thrown violently across the room, slamming onto the desk and then slipping to the floor. On her hands and knees Lucy crawled to him. Frantically, she felt for a pulse. Touching something warm and sticky she jerked her hand back, as if she'd touched fire. She clutched her hands together in front of her, they were icy. Her teeth were chattering, she realized. There was another burst of gunfire, and she crawled under the desk.

She pulled her knees up against her chest and wrapped her trembling arms tight around them, hugging herself. She heard small, whimpering noises, and for a moment she thought a kitten or puppy had somehow gotten trapped with her. She had actually started feeling around for the poor, frightened thing in order to comfort it when she realized she was making the noises herself. She pressed her lips tight together and concentrated on breathing, just breathing, one breath at a time.

A loud crash made her jump, she felt as if her heart would leap out of her body. Then machine-gun fire was raking the room. It was so loud she involuntarily covered her ears with her hands and she smelled something like Fourth of July fireworks. The machine-gun staccato ended with a loud crack, and Lucy felt the floor shake as something heavy fell. Suddenly, there was a bright, white light.

She could hear voices. They seemed to be coming from very far away.

"She's starting to come around."

"I want to interview her, before you take her away."

"I can't let you do that . . ."

Lucy stirred, rolling her head from side to side. She tried to raise herself up, but she couldn't. She was wrapped up in something. Finally, it occurred to her that she could open her eyes.

"Well, hello sunshine."

She blinked, recognizing Lieutenant Horowitz. "Wha'?" she asked.

"You're going to be OK." Another person, this one in a blue uniform, came into view, leaning over her. "We're taking you to the hospital to check you out, but right now it looks like you'll be home for Christmas."

Lucy closed her eyes, only to hear Horowitz's voice.

"Mrs. Stone! I have some questions. . . ."

CHAPTER
TWENTY-TWO

Special Edition
The Pennysaver

Tinker's Cove, Maine
December 26th

Two Killed in Drug Raid
By Edward J. Stillings

TINKER'S COVE — Two men were killed and a Tinker's Cove police officer was wounded in a dramatic Christmas Eve shootout at a Cove Road lobster pound owned by Claude Rousseau, 63. The two dead men were identified as Jean-Jacques Rousseau, 42, of Tinker's Cove and Raymond "Fatman" Norris, 23, of Boston, Mass. Tinker's Cove Police Lt. Thomas Scott, 34, was wounded and remains in stable condition at Memorial Hospital in Portland. Also injured in the raid was *Pen-*

nysaver reporter Lucy Stone, who was treated for a dislocated shoulder at Memorial Hospital and released.

"From the evidence we have so far, it looks as if Norris shot the other two men with an Uzi machine gun," said State Police Detective Lt. C. G. Horowitz. "Norris was killed by a SWAT team member."

A fourth man, Eduardo Reyes, 20, of Boston, Mass., was taken into custody and will most likely be arraigned on Monday. Charges against him have not yet been completely determined, but will include illegal possession of one or more firearms, said Horowitz.

Horowitz said charges are also pending against Scott, who had been under surveillance for several months by the state police special crimes unit. Unit investigators allege that Scott accepted bribes and engaged in drug trafficking while he was acting chief of the Tinker's Cove Police Department. Police are also investigating allegations that Scott murdered Tucker Whitney, 20, of Tinker's Cove earlier this month.

Horowitz said the drug task force was alerted when Norris and Reyes were spotted by a New Hampshire toll collector who noticed their unique automobile. "It was a

Mercedes, top of the line, really loaded, and you don't see a lot of those, at least not this time of year," said Fred W. Smithers, a member of the Classic Car Club of Portsmouth, N.H.

Drug task-force members monitored the pair's progress, notifying the special crimes unit when they appeared headed for Tinker's Cove.

"When Scott, Norris, and Reyes all gathered at Rousseau's Lobster Pound, we knew we had to act fast or lose them," said State Police Capt. Willard Penfield, commander of the drug task force. "It was getting late in the day, and we were losing daylight. We decided to call in the SWAT team."

Tinker's Cove residents watched in amazement as numerous state police vehicles sped through town, with sirens blaring, en route to the lobster pound. Crowd control became a problem for officials as curious onlookers, including a large group of teens who had been attending a pool party at the nearby home of TV star Norah Hemmings, gathered on Smith Heights Road. Hemmings was unavailable for comment.

Charles Canaday, 41, who lives at 151 Smith Heights Road, said he was astonished to see SWAT team members in his backyard.

"I was taking out the garbage and saw what I thought were soldiers, dressed in camouflage and carrying weapons, trotting down my driveway. For a minute I thought it was World War III," said Canady.

The SWAT team cordoned off the lobster pound and set up spotlights, which were immediately shot out by machine-gun fire from Norris.

"We called for replacements, but we knew that was going to take a while, so we improvised with vehicle headlights and fired tear-gas canisters," said Penfield. "Norris ran for cover and one of our snipers had a clear shot and took it. Once Norris went down, Reyes immediately surrendered."

Team members entered the lobster-pound office, where they found the wounded Scott manacled to a pipe with his own handcuffs. Stone was found, unconscious but otherwise apparently unharmed, beneath a large desk. Rousseau's body was also found; both he and Scott appeared to have suffered wounds from machine-gun fire. Norris was killed by a single bullet to the head.

Officials said that more indictments are

expected as the investigation is still in its preliminary stages and will continue.

"We're especially interested in determining what role the Rousseau family played," said Horowitz.

Interviewed at home on Christmas Day, Stone insisted she was an innocent bystander caught in events beyond her control. "I was just picking up some lobsters for Christmas dinner," she said.

CHAPTER
TWENTY-THREE

New Year's Eve

A week later, Lucy's arm and shoulder were still strapped, so she was a passenger in the Subaru while Elizabeth drove. Even though she had a learner's permit, Lucy hadn't had much time to take her daughter driving, so she figured this was a good opportunity for her to get some practice.

"You're doing really great," she said in an encouraging tone of voice as they crept along Main Street. "Now turn on your signal and turn here — I need to go to the post office."

Elizabeth signaled left and turned right, picking up speed and heading directly for the brick post-office building.

"Brake!" shrieked Lucy, and the car lurched to a sudden stop, straddling two parking spaces.

"Sorry about that," said Elizabeth, who was checking her teeth in the rearview mirror. "I get them confused. Which is the gas?"

"The one on the right," said Lucy, opening the door. She wasn't sure which was more dangerous: the shootout at the lobster pound or teaching her own daughter to drive.

She reached back in the car for her purse and when she straightened up, smiled to see Sue leading her little group of daycare kids. They looked like peas in a pod, each child holding tight to a chunky, knotted rope. Bringing up the rear was a young woman Lucy didn't recognize, pushing an oversize baby carriage stuffed with several snow-suited toddlers.

"Hi!" Sue greeted her. "How are you feeling?"

"Much better. I didn't need any pain pills today."

"Kids, you know Mrs. Stone. Sometimes she helps us at the center."

"Hi, Justin. Harry. Emily. Matthew. Did you all have a nice Christmas?"

The kids smiled and nodded, and Emily held out her hands to show off her new dragon mittens.

"Granny made them," she said, opening and closing the dragon's mouth and revealing his hot pink tongue.

"Very nice," said Lucy.

"And this is my new assistant, Casey Wilson," said Sue, indicating a petite young woman who was adjusting Harry's hat.

"Hiya," said Casey, giving Lucy a big smile.

"I don't see Will," said Lucy. "What's happening with him?"

"Steffie's gone home to her folks, in New Jersey." Sue lowered her voice, mindful of the children. "I think she's going to divorce Tom. They weren't that happy, anyway. And now with all that's happened, she's definitely not sticking by her man."

"I don't blame her," said Lucy. "He's bad news. She ought to make a clean break and start over."

"I think she will," said Sue. "She was pretty shook-up. Not quite the same Steffie. Said she was shifting her priorities, and now Will's going to be number one."

"Well, maybe some good will come out of this thing. But if you ask me, I can't quite believe little Miss Goody Two-shoes didn't know what her husband was doing all along. I still haven't forgiven her for bringing those leaflets to the cookie exchange."

"He was pretty controlling," said Sue, with a shrug. "I suspected all along that he was abusive. She even had a restraining order out on him around Thanksgiving."

Lucy's chin dropped as she digested this information.

"You never told me."

"Oops!" Sue's hand flew to her mouth. "Time to go, kids. I hear the bells. That means it's time for lunch."

Lucy watched for a moment as the little procession made its way across the parking lot, recalling how sad the noontime bells had sounded on the day she'd learned of Tucker's death. Today, she thought they sounded hopeful. Ringing out the old year and ringing in the new.

She turned and went inside the post office, pausing at the letter slot, to check that she had all of Toby's college applications. She had just shoved them through the slot when she noticed Marge, also holding a handful of envelopes.

"College applications?" asked Lucy, noticing that Marge looked better than she had in a long time. There was color in her cheeks, and she seemed to have her energy back.

Marge nodded. "He got them done in the nick of time."

"Same here," said Lucy. "Did you have a nice Christmas?"

"Sure did." Marge nodded. "Barney's a lot happier these days. He says getting rid of Tom Scott was the best Christmas present he got!"

"I guess Tom will be going to jail for a long while — Ted says the Rousseaus are only too happy to cooperate and will testify against him. They want to clear the family name."

Lucy pushed open the door and held it for Marge, who paused on the stoop to wave to a passing car.

It was the Cummings family: Steve, Lee, and the girls, driving by in their big sport utility. Lucy also raised her hand in a wave.

"Happy New Year!" shouted Lee, waving out the window. Steve beeped the horn.

"Happy New Year!" called out Marge and Lucy.

"Do you have any special plans for tonight?" asked Marge.

"Actually, the kids are all sleeping over at friends' houses, so Bill and I are planning some cuddle-and-bubble time — he's got a bottle of champagne chilling in the fridge."

"Good for you!" laughed Marge, getting in her car. "Barney's got a six-pack and a video called *Rolling Thunder*."

"Happy New Year!" called Lucy, as she watched Marge back out.

When she pulled open the door to the

Subaru, Elizabeth handed her another letter.

"I found it after you got out," she said.

"You couldn't have brought it in? You just sat here like a lump?"

"Oh." Elizabeth looked at her blankly. "I was listening to my new tape — the Diskettes."

Lucy sighed and took the envelope.

She had just bought a stamp when she noticed Franny Small standing in the corner clutching a letter to her chest, apparently in a state of shock.

"Franny, what's the matter?" she asked. "Did you get bad news?"

"No." Franny's eyes were huge. "It's good news. Really good news."

Franny held out the letter and Lucy took it.

"It's from Neiman Marcus!" she exclaimed, scanning the text. "They want ten thousand pieces of your jewelry!"

"Do you believe it?" Franny's face was glowing. "That's a hundred-thousand-dollar order."

"Wow."

"And the letter says they plan to put them in their catalog next year and anticipate placing further orders."

"That's great, but Franny, how are you

going to do it? Can you make ten thousand pieces of jewelry all by yourself?"

"Don't be silly." Franny's curls shook as she nodded her head. "I'm going to go right over to that economic development agency that's opened in Gilead and get myself what they call a start-up loan. Then I'm going to hire some of those folks who lost their crafts businesses in the fire and put them to work. While they're making the jewelry, I'm going to go out and see who else wants to buy it."

She pointed to the letter.

"If you notice, Neiman Marcus didn't mention anything about exclusive rights. That means I can sell to other customers."

She narrowed her eyes.

"This could be the start of something big."

She looked up.

"Listen, Lucy, I'm sorry, but I don't have time to talk right now. I've got to make some phone calls."

Openmouthed, Lucy watched as Franny bustled off. Then, remembering her errand, she looked down at the letter in her hand. It was the application to Toby's first choice college, Coburn University. She attached a stamp and, crossing her fingers, slipped it through the slot. Then she returned to the car and, saying a little prayer, took her place in the passenger seat.

"Okay, Elizabeth. Look over your shoulder and make sure it's clear. Then, put the shift in reverse, take your foot off the brake. . . ."

"Mom, my foot's not on the brake."

Lucy pressed her hands together to stop the trembling and took a deep breath.

"We'll start over. First, make sure your foot is on the brake. Then, look over your shoulder . . ."

SANTA'S THUMBPRINTS

Lucy always brings these cookies to the cookie exchange.

1 C shortening
1/2 C granulated sugar
1/2 C brown sugar
1 egg
1/2 t vanilla
1/2 t almond extract
1/2 t each baking soda, salt
1 1/2 C uncooked oatmeal
2 C flour
6 oz semisweet chocolate chips

Beat shortening, add sugars, beat til fluffy. Add egg and extracts, mix well. Stir in flour, baking soda, salt, and oatmeal. Shape dough into small balls about the size of a walnut, place on baking sheet, and press hollow in top of each cookie.

Bake at 375 degrees for 10–12 minutes.

Melt chocolate and spoon into center of each cookie. Chill until firm.

Makes about 3 dozen.

SAND TARTS

My Aunt Helen, who was a lot like Miss Tilley, used to bake these cookies every Christmas. I always think of her when I make them.

Cream 1/2 C butter

Add:

1 C sugar
2 egg yolks (beaten)
1 T milk
1/2 t vanilla

Beat mixture until light.

Sift together:

1 1/2 C flour
1 t baking powder
1/2 t salt

Add to first mixture and blend well. Chill for several hours. Roll dough very thin and cut with star cookie cutter. Place on buttered baking sheets and a split, blanched almond in center of each cookie. Brush with unbeaten egg white and sprinkle with mixture of 1 T sugar and 1/4 t cinnamon. Bake at 375 degrees for 10 minutes.

ABOUT THE AUTHOR

Leslie Meier lives with her family in Massachusetts. Leslie loves to hear from her readers and you may write to her c/o Kensington Publishing. Please include a self-addressed stamped envelope if you wish a response.